A Sourcebook of Learning Activities

A Sourcebook of
Learning Activities

LeRoy Ford

BROADMAN PRESS
Nashville, Tennessee

© Copyright 1984 ● Broadman Press
All rights reserved
4234-30

ISBN: 0-8054-3430-5
Dewey Decimal Classification: 268.6
Subject Heading: TEACHING
Library of Congress Catalog Card Number: 83-27223

Printed in the United States of America

Library of Congress Cataloging in Publication Data

Ford, LeRoy.
    A sourcebook of learning activities.

    1. Activity programs in Christian education—
Handbooks, manuals, etc. I. Title.
BV1536.5.F67   1984   268'.6   83-27223
ISBN 0-8054-3430-5 (pbk.)

Contents

Introduction 7

Section I: Activities to Develop Understanding 11

Section II: Activities to Develop Attitudes and
            Values 56

Section III: Activities to Develop Memory and Recall
             Abilities 94

Introduction

Teaching involves three processes: (1) stating learning goals and objectives, (2) designing appropriate learning activities, and (3) evaluating progress.

Many teachers can state goals and objectives but find it hard to create learning activities. They ask, "After we've stated a goal, *how* do we involve the pupils actively in reaching the goal?"

This book provides help. It presents 101 basic learning activities classified according to age group and the kind of learning involved. Each includes two or more variations which teachers may "link" or "chain" onto the first one. In this sense, the book contains over 300 learning activities.

"Activity linking" or "chaining" helps teachers build many activities onto a single one. In activity linking, a teacher links onto an initial activity other related activities dealing with the same subject or goal. The linked activities may deal with the same kind of learning—understanding, for example. Or they may cross lines and include activities which deal with both understanding and attitudes.

The following example of activity linking or chaining deals with "What Church Means." Notice that the numerous and varied activities deal with the same subject. The teacher first thought of activity number 1, then asked, "What other activities can I build onto that one?" Most of the activities shown relate to the goal of *understanding* what church means. Some, however, (nos. 5, 10, and 11) help develop *attitudes* toward the church.

In some cases, one activity grows logically out of the preceding one. Numbers 1 through 4 grow naturally one out of the other.

Use of the process of activity linking or chaining can help teachers get the most out of a single good idea.

Each activity description includes the following sections:

Purpose: This section states the educational purpose for which one may use the activity. For example, given activities may help the learner generalize, recall information, solve problems, organize values, interpret meanings, transfer learning, and so on.

Activity: This section describes the specific action the learner takes when doing an activity. For example, activities may involve working a crossword puzzle, arranging in order a set of items, identifying evidences of application or violation of principles, writing poems or stories, organizing a project, and so on.

Example: This section presents one or more concrete examples dealing with a subject. It presents specific "germ ideas" which one may adapt to a large number of subjects.

Variations: This section includes a list of one or more related learning activities which a teacher may link or chain onto the initial one.

Cautions: Occasionally a list of cautions appears when experience has brought to light certain pitfalls in the use of an activity. For example, the description might say, "Caution: Use soluble ink when writing on the transparency. You may need to erase part of the design and revise it."

The variations may involve increasing complexity from one level of learning to another. They may give ideas for moving from *knowing* to *feeling*. They may simply give ideas for doing a variety of things at the same learning level.

The book classifies the activities according to (1) the kind of learning and (2) the age group(s) with which one may want to use the activity. The following categories suggest the kind of activities:

Memory-Recall activities call only for practice in recalling from memory facts and information learned before.

Understanding activities include the lower levels of understanding (such as comprehension) and the higher levels of understanding (such as problem solving and evaluation).

Attitudes and Values activities involve those levels of learning related to attitudes and values (organizing one's value system, for example). Some involve simpler levels (such as seeing the worth or value of something).

The following categories give a general idea as to which age group

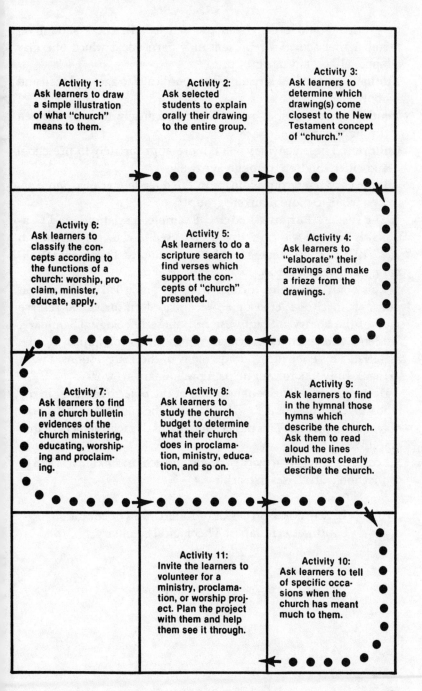

Activity 1:
Ask learners to draw a simple illustration of what "church" means to them.

Activity 2:
Ask selected students to explain orally their drawing to the entire group.

Activity 3:
Ask learners to determine which drawing(s) come closest to the New Testament concept of "church."

Activity 6:
Ask learners to classify the concepts according to the functions of a church: worship, proclaim, minister, educate, apply.

Activity 5:
Ask learners to do a scripture search to find verses which support the concepts of "church" presented.

Activity 4:
Ask learners to "elaborate" their drawings and make a frieze from the drawings.

Activity 7:
Ask learners to find in a church bulletin evidences of the church ministering, educating, worshiping and proclaiming.

Activity 8:
Ask learners to study the church budget to determine what their church does in proclamation, ministry, education, and so on.

Activity 9:
Ask learners to find in the hymnal those hymns which describe the church. Ask them to read aloud the lines which most clearly describe the church.

Activity 11:
Invite the learners to volunteer for a ministry, proclamation, or worship project. Plan the project with them and help them see it through.

Activity 10:
Ask learners to tell of specific occasions when the church has meant much to them.

9

or groups would profit from the activity. Teachers should remember that activities represent only germ ideas which one may adapt to almost any age group.

Adults: These activities relate more specifically to ages eighteen and above.

Youth: These activities relate more specifically to ages thirteen through seventeen.

Children: These activities relate more appropriately to preschool and older children (through age twelve.)

Indexes to age groups appear in the outside margins. Some activities relate to more than one group.

The format **(Purpose, Activity, Example, Variations,** and **Cautions)** is original with me. It was first used in class assignments in 1977-1978 in courses at the Southwestern Baptist Theological Seminary, Fort Worth, Texas.

This book, using this format, was first published for validation purposes in 1979-1980. Copies were placed on the closed reserve shelf of the library at Southwestern Baptist Theological Seminary. Students and teachers provided helpful ideas for improving the material. This book incorporates many of their suggestions. I want to thank Judy Rex for her help on preliminary art work.

Development of the book was one of the objectives stated in my sabbatic leave proposal for 1979-1980. The sabbatic leave report notes its completion. This publication marks the achievement of that objective.

I coined the terms *activity chaining* and *activity linking* in 1978 in connection with classes in teaching.

LeRoy Ford, professor of foundations of education
Southwestern Baptist Theological Seminary

Section I
Activities to Develop
Understanding

Purpose: This activity should help learners conceptualize.

Activity: Present to the student a list of items and a corresponding list of functions or characteristics associated with them. Ask the learners to match the items.

Example: Provide learners with copies of the following matching exercise. Ask them to draw lines connecting the related items.

1. Farmers   cook our bread
2. Millers   buy bread for us to eat
3. Bakers   plant wheat seeds
4. Grocers   grind wheat into flour
5. Parents   sell bread in their stores[1]

Variations: Link onto this example such other activities as these:

1. Substitute pictures for the items in the first column.
2. Ask learners to arrange in chronological order the processes in the second column. Ask: What happens before the farmer plants the seeds? (he plows) What happens after parents buy the bread? (we eat)

CHILDREN

11

Purpose: This activity should help learners develop problem-solving and analytical skills and improve skills in composition.

Activity: Present the learners with a scrambled set of drawings which represent events in a study. Ask them to arrange the events in the order in which they feel they happened in the story. Then ask each learner to tell the story in his own words.

Example: Cut out the drawings in the following picture story. Scramble them. Then ask the learners to arrange them in the order in which they feel the events occurred.

Variations: Link to the example such activities as these:

1. Ask the learners to "write" a children's book and illustrate with the pictures.
2. Omit some essential pictures from a story. Ask the learners to decide which important events you have omitted and to supply drawings to complete the story.

13

Purpose: This activity should help learners develop analytical and problem solving abilities and increase composition skills.

Activity: Display a picture of an event. Ask learners to tell what they think happened just before the picture was made and to project what they think will happen next.

Example: 1. Display the following picture. Ask, What do you think happened before? What do you think happened after?

YOUTH

Variations: Link to the example such activities as these:
1. "Force" the sequence back further by continuing to ask, And what do you think happened before *that*?
2. Ask the learners themselves to draw an original picture. Ask them to describe to another person what happened before and after.

CHILDREN

Purpose: This activity should help learners transfer learning into new situations.

Activity: Enclose in a container (sack, waste basket) a collection of items related to a profession, occupation, or other activity. Ask students to feel inside the container and, by touch alone, identify the items and tell how one would use them in a given kind of work.

Example: Place in a large paper sack the following items: A Band-Aid, an eraser, a piece of chalk, a pair of scissors, some seeds such as dried beans, a Bible, a harmonica or other small musical instrument, and other items.

Ask the learners to feel inside the bag and locate items which the following would use in their work: a doctor, a teacher, a musician. The ask, How would the person use the item?

Variations: Link onto the example other activities, such as these:

1. Ask a pupil to reach into the bag and describe the item he touches. Ask other learners to tell what the pupil describes and tell who would use it and how.
2. Display a large collection of items on a table. Ask the pupils to sort them according to which ones medical, agricultural, evangelistic, music, and education missionaries would use.
3. Blindfold the learners. Ask three of them to handle the same object. The first tells its size; the second, its shape; the third, how it feels. Ask all learners to guess what the object is and explain how a certain kind of missionary might use it

YOUTH

CHILDREN

Purpose: This activity should help learners generalize.

Activity: Provide a list of generalizations (such as animals, sports, occupations, gems, plants) and a list of three or four letters of the alphabet. Ask the learners to provide examples in each category beginning with the given letters.

Example: Give learner a copy of the following chart. Ask him or her to fill in the boxes with words which begin with the letters shown. Examples appear under the letter *P*.

	P	B	L	O
HOUSEHOLD FURNISHINGS	POT			
FRUITS	PLUM			
OCCUPATIONS	PLUMBER			

YOUTH

Ask groups of learners to compile their words and share them with the larger group.

Variations: Link onto this example such other activities as these:
1. Reverse the process. Provide the names of items and ask learners to provide the generalization.
2. Present several words which represent degrees of generalization. Ask learner to rank the words in order from most general to least general. For example: Apples, food, fruit, apples.

CHILDREN

Purpose: This activity should help learners generalize.

Activity: Present to the learner several sets of three or four words each. One item does not belong. Ask, Which item does not belong?

Example: On the chalkboard write the following sets of words:

oak	pen	diamond
cedar	spade	ruby
bean	pencil	garnet
poplar	chalk	golf
light	automobile	horse
yellow	wheelbarrow	dog
amber	bus	man
violet	airplane	run

Ask the learners to circle the word which does not belong, and to explain why.

Variations: Link or chain onto this example such other activities as these:

1. Ask them to tell the general term for the three words in each list.
2. Ask learners themselves to make up several sets of words. One word in each set should not belong.
3. Use proper names of countries, people, and so on. For example: Shakespeare, Roosevelt, Eisenhower, Kennedy; Africa, Atlantic, Asia, Australia; Bonne, Zaire, Chicago, Moscow.
4. Use sets of pictures instead of words.

17

Purpose: This activity should help learners conceptualize.

Activity: On the chalkboard, write the name of an occupation or profession or the name of a well-known person. Ask the students to brainstorm verbs which tell what the person does.

Example: On the chalkboard, write the word *doctor*. Ask the pupils to call out things a doctor does. Write these on the chalkboard. One group suggested these verbs:

Doctor

heals	consults
operates	refers
prescribes	visits
diagnoses	studies
writes	

YOUTH

Variations: Link or chain onto this example such other activities as these:

1. Ask learners to classify the verbs according to what the doctor does to prepare himself and what he actually does with the patient.

2. Ask learners to write a job description for a doctor. Assume they need to hire a doctor for a clinic for the underprivileged. What would they expect him to do?

CHILDREN

Purpose: This activity should help learners develop creative writing skills.

Activity: Ask students to create their own cartoon dialogue.

Example: Provide each learner with a copy of the unfinished cartoon shown below. Ask them to decide upon two characters to include in the dialogue. Then ask them to write into the cartoon "balloons" the dialogue and draw stick figures to show the action.

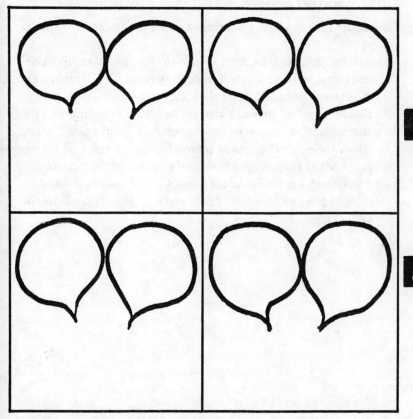

YOUTH

OLDER CHILDREN

Variations: Link or chain onto this example such other activities as these:
1. As a stimulus provide the speech for one of the characters. Ask learners to provide responses for the other character.
2. Suggest to the learners a Bible story which includes two characters. Ask them to write the story using cartoon dialogue.

Purpose: This activity should help learners develop analytical and problem-solving abilities.

Activity: Present a cartoon case study in which one character presents a one-liner case. The learner composes the other character's response.

Example: On the chalkboard draw a cartoon similar to the illustration. Ask learners in small groups to determine an answer and write it into the "balloon."

Variations: Link or chain onto this example such other activities as these:

1. Ask learners to draw their own cartoons and make up a one-liner case related to their own concerns. The learners exchange cartoons and determine answers.

2. Divide learners into small groups. Ask them to assume that the character who answers can answer only with a Bible verse. Allow time for a Scripture search for the verses. Call for reports or call for learners to write the verses into the cartoon.

3. Ask learners to study the account of Jesus' temptation and locate the places where Jesus answered with a quotation from the Old Testament.

21

Purpose: This activity should help learners comprehend what they read and express themselves through composition.

Activity: Ask learners to express in limerick form something they read.

Example: Ask learners to express in limerick form the story of the change of Saul's name to Paul. Allow them to share their work with other group members.

For example, one learner wrote this limerick:

> There was a young man named Saul.
> Who despised Christians most of all.
> He believed himself right
> 'Til he really "saw the light"
> And became the apostle named Paul.

Variations: Link to this example such other activities as these:

YOUTH

1. Instead of having learners write the entire limerick, furnish them with the first line and let them complete the limerick. For example: "Nicodemus came to Jesus by night."
2. Ask learner to do a Bible search to find the Bible verse which prompted each line.

Purpose: This activity should help learners develop problem-solving and analytical skills.

Activity: Ask the learners to work through a maze and to make a list of the things they did mentally as they worked through it.

Example: Arrange the chairs in a room so as to form a simple maze, such as the following.

```
hh  ↓  hhhhhhhhhhhhhhhhhhhh
h   '          h              h
h       hhhhh        hhhhhh    h
h         h           h        h
h         h   hhhhhh   h       
h         h     h       h   →  
h         h     h        hhhhh
h                              h
hhhhhhhhhhhhhhhhhhhhhhhhhhhh
```

Blindfold two group members. Ask them to find their way out of the maze as other group members observe and make notes. The blindfolded persons may talk to each other and share what they have discovered about an escape route.

Ask the blindfolded persons to describe the mental activity they used in escaping the maze. Then lead the group to summarize the steps involved in solving problems (get the facts, relate the facts one to another, make a decision, take action, evaluate, try out).

Variations: Link onto this example such other activities as this one:
1. Present this problem: You are to develop a plan for doing a telephone survey in a large city. Ask: How would you go about developing the plan? What similarities do you see between working through a maze and working out a plan to do the telephone survey?
2. Lead the group to try to solve this problem using the steps in problem solving: How can we improve our church visitation program?

Purpose: This activity should help learners comprehend meanings.

Activity: Ask learners to find literary interpretations of well-known Bible verses, proverbs, or other expressions of great thought.

Example: On the chalkboard, write "Lo, I am with you alway." Ask learners to suggest titles or lines from hymns or popular songs which reflect the idea. (One group listed these hymn titles: "What a Friend We Have in Jesus," "No, Never Alone," and so on.)

Variations: Link or chain onto this example such other activities as these:

1. Ask learners to decide which line in the song best expresses the thought.
2. Reverse the process. Provide a line from a song. Ask learners to recall a Bible verse which expresses the idea.

YOUTH

24

Purpose: This activity should help learners comprehend meanings.

Activity: Ask the learners to match synonyms.

Example: Provide each learner with a copy of the following matching exercise. Simple words appear in the left-hand column. More complex words appear as synonymns on the right-hand side. Ask learners to match the lists by drawing a line from each word to its synonymn.

hole	adoration
show	suspend
worship	aperture
hang	gigantic
big	exhibit

Variations: Link onto this example such other activities as these:

1. Ask each learner to think of a multisyllable word which has a one-syllable synonymn. Ask other learners to guess what he had in mind. (Example: diminutive—small.)
2. Ask learners to build the words into a crossword puzzle.

YOUTH

Purpose: This activity should help learners to comprehend meanings.

Activity: Ask learners to discover a word or phrase which summarizes a given unit of study or a lesson.

Example: To introduce a unit of study on "Ye Are My Witnesses," place on the floor large cutouts of the following letters:

H E S V N E A R I Y T C T R S I B O J

Ask learners to discover what the letters say when rearranged. Provide clues when necessary: the last three letters make up one of the words; it contains three words; at one point every other letter spells a word. Ask them to rearrange the letters to spell out the words. (Answer: "Every Christian's Job")

Variations: Link onto this example such other examples as this:

1. Provide a set of summary words. Ask learners to choose which word best summarizes the unit.
2. Show the summary word in two or three languages other than English. Ask learners to discover what they mean.

Purpose: This activity should help learners organize given material according to a systematic plan.

Activity: Ask learners to discover how a given literary piece reflects a predetermined set of ideas.

Example: On the chalkboard write the following words:

diary	microscope
psychiatrist	animated cartoon
mother	mirror
	spotlight

Then ask each learner, or group of learners, to make a list of ways the Bible is like each of the words. (For example: Mirror—the Bible shows us what we really are like.) Call for reports.[2]

Variations: Link onto this example such other activities as these:

1. Ask learners to think of other words which would complete the sentence: "The Bible is like a _____." Then continue the process as described.

2. Reverse the process: Ask learners to tell in several statements something the Bible does. (For example: It serves as a lamp to our feet.) Then let group members think of the word or generalization which the statements call to mind. (For example, a guide.)

Purpose: This activity should develop verbal composition skills.

Activity: Ask a question which calls for the person to make a value judgment about an experience. Or simply ask for her opinion about a problem or event. Then ask, "Why?"—to which the learner replies with "because . . ." (She elaborates the situation, in effect, outlining her viewpoints for use as a basis for writing a composition.)

Examples: 1. Ask, "Did you have a good time on your vacation in Maine?" The pupil may answer, "No, it was a complete disappointment." Then ask, "Why?" The pupil may answer, "Well, the cottage didn't live up to the advertising, the people next door drove us crazy, and everything was so expensive we spent more money than we should have." Ask the learner to organize her responses and write a composition based on the responses in this "why-and-because" exercise.[3]

YOUTH

2. Ask, "Do Baptists believe in baptism by immersion?" The pupil may answer "No." Then ask, Why? Follow through with the "why and because" exercise until the pupil has an outline.

Variations: Link onto the example activities such as these:
1. Begin by asking a question about a picture. For example, "What is this person doing in the picture?" "Why?" Proceed through the process described in the example.

OLDER CHILDREN

2. Ask the learner to make speeches instead of writing compositions.

Purpose: This activity should help the learner develop problem-solving and analysis skills and to develop concepts.

Activity: Present to the learner a diagram or picture which shows a process of a concept in action. Ask the learner two questions: What happens in this picture? Why does it happen?

Example: Display the following picture which illustrates the concept that hot air rises and cold air displaces it. Ask, What do you see happening? Why does it happen?

ADULTS

YOUTH

Variations: Link onto this example such other activities as these:
1. Present the same picture, but show the arrows going in opposite direction. Ask, What is wrong in this picture? Why?
2. Ask learners to suggest two or three other examples of situations where something warm rises or something cold descends. (Water in a lake, heat in an oven, air in a refrigerator.)
3. Show a picture of a refrigerator with the door open. Ask, Where would the cold air go?

Purpose: This activity should help learners develop analytical and problem-solving abilities.

Activity: Present two statements which seem to conflict with each other. Ask the learners to reconcile the statements or to explain why the statements cannot be reconciled.

ADULTS

Example: Write the following on the chalkboard. Ask, how do you reconcile the two statements? Can you reconcile them?

All learning comes through experience.

For I neither received it of man, neither was I taught it, but by the revelation of Jesus Christ.

Variations: Link to this example such other activities as these:

YOUTH

1. Ask group members in groups of two to discuss the question, Can we classify as learning that which happens as a result of divine revelation? Why? Call for reports. Would Paul classify as learning through experience the significant happening on the road to Damascus? Why?
2. Ask learners to brainstorm examples of kinds of experiences from which we learn. (They may suggest reading, seeing films, going on a trip, listening to a recording, acting in a play, taking part in a worship service.) Then ask them to classify the experiences as to whether the experience came *through* someone else or was experienced directly. Then ask, Can we classify reading a book as an experience? Why? Why not?

Purpose: This activity should help learners transfer to new situations what they have learned; to generalize.

Activity: Call out a list of items. Ask learners to indicate when in the list you switch from one concept to another.

Example: Read aloud the following two lists of items. Ask the learners to raise their hands when you switch from the specific to the generalization in each list.

ADULTS

1	2	3
run	faith	red
walk	hope	blue
write	love	green
build	joy	yellow
say	fruit	color
verbs	results	hue
adjectives		tint
adverbs		

YOUTH

(In number 1, the switch comes between say and verbs—switching from individual verbs to the generalization. In number 2, the switch comes between joy and fruit. Fruit is the generalization under which the Scripture classifies the others.)

Variations: Link or chain onto this example such other activities as these:

OLDER CHILDREN

1. Ask individual learners to make up their own lists related to the unit of study. Then ask them in groups of four to read their lists. Others in the group determine the switching point.
2. Read a list in which you do not make a switch. Let group members discover for themselves that no switch is made.

Purpose: This activity should help learners interpret and comprehend principles and concepts.

Activity: Provide students with a set of principles or definitions. Ask them to underline what they consider to be the key word in each statement and to define the word.

ADULTS

Examples: 1. Underline and define key words in these verses: "Blessed be ye poor: for yours is the kingdom of God. Blessed are ye that hunger now: for ye shall be filled. Blessed are ye that weep now: for ye shall laugh. Blessed are ye, when men shall hate you, and when they shall separate you from their company, and shall reproach you, and cast out your name as evil, for the Son of man's sake" (Luke 6:20-22).

2. Underline the key word in each of the following principles of teaching:

YOUTH

Arrange for learners to observe leaders who set the right example—who exemplify the attitude.

Involve learners in activities which call for active response.

Provide activities in which the learner changes (translates) ideas into new forms.

Provide immediate knowledge of results when a learner responds.

Involve the learner in activities which call for him to use (or transfer) the learning to new situations.

Variations: Link activities like this onto the examples:

1. After the activity just described, call out key words and ask learners to reconstruct the entire statement in their own words.

Purpose: This activity should help learners develop analytical and problem-solving skills.

Activity: Display a picture in which something essential is missing. Ask, What is missing in this picture?

Example: Assume that the following picture was made *before* the advent of the electric motor but *after* the invention of the steam engine. What is missing in the picture? (no smokestack)

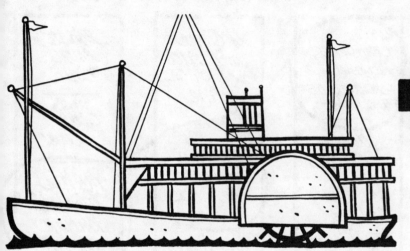

Variations: Link activities like these onto this example:

1. Show two or three pictures, only one of which is accurate. Ask, Which of these pictures was made before the electric motor but after the advent of the steam engine?
2. Display a picture which includes all the essential elements. Ask, What would happen if we removed this part? (What would happen if we removed the smokestack from this tugboat?)
3. Display a picture which includes something which *does not belong.* Ask, What does not belong in this picture?

Purpose: This activity should help learners interpret meanings.

Activity: Ask learners to suggest synonyms or phrases which mean the same as selected words in a statement. Then read the statement in its amplified versions.

Example: On the chalkboard write the following Bible verse. Underline the words indicated. Ask for synonyms or phrases which one could substitute accurately for the underlined portions.

ADULTS

YOUTH

"*I know that my redeemer liveth*"

am convinced beyond the shadow of a doubt	the one who paid the price for me	exist even now
surely believe	he who bought me back	still lives
am assured in my heart	purchased	makes himself known today

Chain the synonyms or phrases together by circling suggested ones as shown in the example so as to form a complete statement. Repeat the process using different combinations of words.

Variations: Link to the example such activities as these:
1. Control the substitutions by requiring one-syllable words.
2. Ask learners to provide phrases based on dictionary definitions of the key words.
3. Ask learners to compare *their* interpretations with the same verse in modern language translations.
4. Ask learners to tell of personal experiences of God's presence.

Caution: Learners tend to suggest single words instead of phrases.

34

Purpose: This activity should help students understand a concept or step.

Activity: Ask students to match a concept or a step in a process with an illustration or an interpretative example of the concept, such as a Bible verse.

Example: Match the following steps in the lesson planning process with the Bible verse which illustrates it.

___ 1. Determine aim	a.	"And he spake . . . unto them in parables" (Matt. 13:3).
___ 2. Relate to unit	b.	"[When] ye ask, . . . ye ask amiss" (Jas. 4:3).
___ 3. Select methods	c.	"Consider the lilies of the field" (Matt. 6:28).
___ 4. Prepare learning aids	d.	"The tree is known by [its] fruit" (Matt. 12:33).
___ 5. Plan for follow through	e.	"Ye have heard that it hath been said, . . . but I say unto you" (Matt. 5:21-22).
___ 6. Evaluate results	f.	"Why call ye me Lord, Lord, and do not the things I say?" (Luke 6:46).

Variations: Link to the example such activities as these:

1. When possible, match the concepts or steps with a *drawing* or picture which represents the idea.
2. Ask learners to find on their own illustrations or statements to place in the second column—thus making *their own* matching game. Then ask them to try out the project with other persons in the group.

Purpose: This activity should help learners develop analytical and problem-solving abilities.

Activity: Ask learners to complete a grid which calls for the learner to explore the possible relationships between sets of givens.

ADULTS

Example: Give each learner a copy of the chart which follows. Ask learners to consider each pair of items and fill in the box with appropriate information. For example, one square relates to "role of head of state" and to "republic." In the box we might write "powers limited by Constitution" and "recommends legislation." Continue this process until a comprehensive survey results. Learners may work in small groups.

YOUTH

	Role of head of state	Role of legislative body	Role of the people
Republic			
Pure Monarchy			
Constitutional Monarchy			

Variations: Link onto the example activities such as these:
1. Raise the level of learning to a more complex level by asking learners to write a report based on the outline.
2. Make word strips of the findings in the activity. Shuffle the strips. Ask learners to place the strips in the appropriate box.

Purpose: This activity helps learners develop communication skills.

Activity: Ask a learner to reproduce a diagram or to make an article relying on oral instructions only, without feedback.

Example: Ask one learner to play the role of the "sender" in a communication experiment. Ask the other members of the group to follow the "sender's" instructions.

Position the sender so that group members cannot see him but can hear him. Give the sender a copy of the following diagram. Ask him to describe the diagram carefully so that other group members can draw one just like it. They may not at any time see the diagram but may converse with the sender. The sender may not watch what the others do.

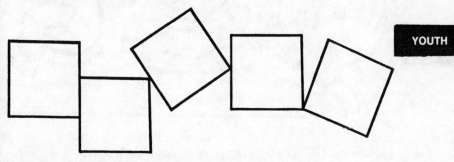

When they finish, show the original diagram.
Guide a discussion based on questions such as these:
1. How did you feel as you tried to draw the diagram?
2. What could the sender have done to help you receive the communication more accurately?
3. Which critical directions did the sender omit?
4. What guidelines for communication can you draw from this activity?[4]

Variations: Link onto the example activities such as these:
1. Ask only one student to reproduce the diagram on the chalk-board in front of the group. Ask the other members to watch, with the questions above in mind.
2. Ask a student to fold a paper hat or a diaper, receiving instructions by telephone from another student.

Caution: Caution the group members to remain silent.

Purpose: This activity should help learners develop comprehension ability.

Activity: Display a series of related pictures. Ask the learners to give a title to the pictures or the series.

Example: Display the following series of pictures. Ask the learners to provide a title for the series from the viewpoint of the Christian life.

ADULTS

YOUTH

TITLE: _____

Variations: Link or chain onto this example such activities as these:

OLDER CHILDREN

1. Instead of titles, ask learners to recall a Bible passage which they might use as a caption.
2. Ask the learners to suggest the title of a hymn (or a line from a hymn) which expresses the idea.
3. For an attitudinal dimension to the activity, ask each learner to tell of growth experiences in his or her own life.
4. After giving a title to the series, ask learners to give titles to individual pictures in the series.

Purpose: This activity should help learners develop analytical and problem-solving abilities.

Activity: Make a significant statement or state an hypothesis. Ask learners to decide whether they agree or disagree with the statement. Why? Why not?

Examples: 1. Ask the students in groups of two to discuss whether they agree or disagree with the following statement: Salvation and conversion mean the same thing. Call for explanations of whether they agree or do not agree.

ADULTS

2. Ask learners whether they agree or disagree with the statement: Teaching is both an art and a science.

Variations: Link to the examples such other activities as these:
1. Ask teams to debate the statements.
2. Ask a learner who agrees with the statement to assume the negative position and present arguments which a "do-not-agree" person might make.

YOUTH

Caution: Some persons who do not understand the reasons for the activity assume that the statements are true even though stated negatively.

Purpose: This activity should help learners comprehend meanings.

Activity: Ask students to suggest in rapid-fire order the synonyms and antonymns for a given word or concept.

Examples: 1. On the chalkboard write the word *democracy*. Ask students to suggest words which we associate with the word, and words which relate to the opposite concept.

For example, students may suggest such words as these:

Democracy

Synonyms and related words:	*Antonyms and opposite ideas:*
republic	dictatorship
the people	aristocracy
majority	slavery
constitutional	kings
law	
individual rights	
freedom	

2. Write on the chalkboard the word *worship*. Ask students to suggest words which mean the same and words which mean the opposite.

Variations: Link or chain onto these examples such activities as these:

1. Ask students to compose a definition of democracy, using the words suggested.
2. Ask, Which words have a negative feel? a positive feel?

Purpose: This activity should help learners develop the ability to comprehend concepts.

Activity: Ask learners to find in several different dictionaries the meanings of a given word. Ask them to list the similarities and differences among the definitions.

Example: Provide a Bible dictionary and several other dictionaries for students to use. Ask them to find and compare meanings of the word *love*. Then ask them to list similarities and differences in the definitions. You may use the following definitions:

Bible dictionary: The power to overcome hostile relationships.

Random House Dictionary: The benevolent affection of God for his creatures or the reverent affection due from them to God.

Webster's Dictionary: To feel reverent adoration for God.

(Note: They will note that one says affection, another adoration; some suggest relationships to God and to fellowman, and so on.)

Variations: Link or chain onto this example such activities as these:
1. Ask students to decide which definition comes closest to the New Testament concept of love (*agape*).
2. Ask students to explain the various kinds of love involved in its meaning (*agape,* brotherly love, *eros,* and so on.)

ADULTS

YOUTH

Purpose: This activity should help the learner develop reading comprehension skills.

Activity: Ask the students to read a paragraph which contains a significant idea. Ask the learners to suggest a title for the paragraph.

Example: Read aloud 1 John 1:1-7. Ask learners to suggest in not more than four or five words a title for the passage.

ADULTS

YOUTH

"That which was from the beginning, which we have heard, which we have seen with our eyes, which we have looked upon, and our hands have handled, of the Word of life; (For the life was manifested, and we have seen *it,* and bear witness, and shew unto you that eternal life, which was with the Father, and was manifested unto us;) That which we have seen and heard declare we unto you, that ye also may have fellowship with us: and truly our fellowship *is* with the Father, and with his Son Jesus Christ. And these things write we unto you, that your joy may be full. This then is the message which we have heard of him, and declare unto you, that God is light, and in him is no darkness at all. If we say that we have fellowship with him, and walk in darkness, we lie, and do not the truth: But if we walk in the light, as he is in the light, we have fellowship one with another, and the blood of Jesus Christ his Son cleanseth us from all sin."

Variations: Link or chain onto this example such activities as these:
1. Ask the learners to find the phrase or word which best expresses what the passage means.
2. Provide three or four possible titles for the passage. Ask learners to select the most appropriate one.

Purpose: This activity should help learners apply in new situations what they have learned.

Activity: Ask the learner to study a given set of materials and determine the mistakes or examples of malpractice.

Examples: Study the following picture. Which principles of hospital visitation have the visitors violated?

ADULTS

YOUTH

OLDER CHILDREN

Variations: Link to the examples such activities as these:

1. Ask learners to give examples of the correct way to visit.
2. Ask learners to "pose" a picture of the correct way, if the subject lends itself to posing.
3. Ask learner to analyze *feelings* or attitudes of each character in the drawing in the example.

Purpose: This activity should help the learner develop comprehension ability.

Activity: Suggest to the student a concept or idea and ask him to translate it into a line drawing.

Examples: On the chalkboard write the word *disorganization*. Ask the pupil to do a line drawing which conveys the concept. For example, he may draw something like this:

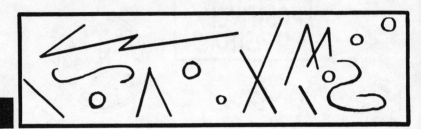

Now write on the chalkboard the word *organization*. Ask the learner to do a line drawing which conveys the concept. For example, he may draw something like this:

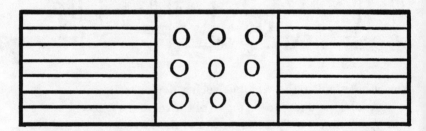

Variations: Link onto this example such other activities as these:
1. Reverse the procedure. Present to the learner a line drawing which represents a concept. Ask him to suggest the concept it conveys.
2. Ask learners to compare drawings made by group members and determine which best illustrates the concept.

Caution: Because of individual differences among learners, some may find it difficult to express ideas in picture form.

Purpose: This activity should help learners develop reading comprehension skills.

Activity: Assign each of several work groups a key word in the resource material they study. (From a political speech, a Bible passage, an essay, or a document such as the Declaration of Independence.) Ask each study group to construct a symbol which conveys what the word means. Provide crayons, modeling clay, and other art materials. Ask for explanations.

ADULTS

Example: On the chalkboard, write the following Bible passage. Then ask work groups to construct a symbol which conveys what the following words mean: *Complete, same mind, selfishness, humility.* Then call for reports before reading the passage aloud. "*Complete* my joy by being of the *same mind,* having the same love, being in full accord and of one mind. Do nothing from *selfishness* or conceit, but in *humility* count others better than yourselves" (Phil. 2:2-3, RSV).

YOUTH

Variations: Link to this example such other activities as these:
1. Ask the learners to choose the key words, then construct the symbols.
2. Provide Bible dictionaries and commentaries to work groups. Ask them to study the word in these Bible helps. Then ask, Does the symbol you prepared convey the same ideas found in the Bible study helps? If not, what would you add or take away?
3. Ask learners to rewrite the material, substituting their symbols for the words.

Purpose: This activity should help learners develop analytical and problem-solving abilities.

Activity: Provide each learner with a readily available resource (magazine or newspaper, for example). Ask them to make a computation based on data they discover there.

Example: Ask learners to bring to class copies of the daily newspaper. Ask them to find what percent or what fraction of the total newspaper is devoted to:

advertisements	comics
classified ads	editorials
international news	local news
society news	statistics
sports	pictures

They may report by percentages or by column inches.[5]

Variations: Link onto this example such other activities as these:
1. Ask learners to select part of the newspaper (classified ads, for example) and do an analysis of it.
2. Change the activity to an attitudinal one by asking, What does your report say about the values of persons in your community? What influences the newspaper to have this ratio of parts? How would you change it? Could the newspaper do it if so desired? What do economics of journalism say about changing the emphases in the newspaper?

Purpose: This activity should help learners comprehend what they read.

Activity: Read aloud a short paragraph which tells a story involving several facts and events. Then ask learners, relying on memory, to answer questions about who, why, where, when, and what as related to the story.

ADULTS

Example: Read to the learners the following story. Then give each a copy of the true-false questions related to the story. Divide the members into groups of three or four. Ask them to share the answers and come to a concensus regarding the facts.

The Story

A businessman had just turned off the lights in the store when a man appeared and demanded money. The owner opened a cash register. The contents of the cash register were scooped up, and the man sped away. A member of the police force was notified promptly.

Statments About the Story

YOUTH

1.	A man appeared after the owner had turned off his store lights	T	F	?
2.	The robber was a *man*.	T	F	?
3.	The man did not demand money.	T	F	?
4.	The man who opened the cash register was the owner.	T	F	?
5.	The store owner scooped up the contents of the cash register and ran away.	T	F	?
6.	Someone opened a cash register.	T	F	?
7.	After the man who demanded the money scooped up the contents of the cash register, he ran away.	T	F	?
8.	While the cash register contained money, the story does not state *how much*.	T	F	?
9.	The robber demanded money of the owner.	T	F	?
10.	The story concerns a series of events in which only three persons are referred to: the owner of the store, a man who demanded money, and a member of the police force.	T	F	?
11.	The following events in the story are true: someone demanded money, a cash register was opened, its contents were scooped up, and a man dashed out of the store.	T	F	?[6]

Variations: Link onto this example such other activities as these:

1. Write a story in such a way that it contains not only facts, but reports a decision or possible answers regarding a problem. After learners recall facts, ask them to arrive at a concensus as to whether the decision was right. (This raises the activity to a higher level of learning.)

2. Display a picture for two or three minutes. Then ask learners to answer questions related to it. For example, was the boy going to or from the bus stop?

Purpose: This activity should help learners develop problem-solving ability.

Activity: Present the learners with a short case study involving a personal conflict situation. Ask learners to determine what should be done in the situation.

Example: Read aloud the following case study. Ask one group of learners to decide which principles of Christian family living have been violated. Ask another group to decide how they would counsel the parents in this case.

Dear Folks,

Thank you for everything, but I am going to go to Chicago and try to start some kind of new life.

You asked me why I did those things and why I gave you two so much trouble and the answer is so easy for f me to give you, but I am wondering if you will understand.

Remember when I was about six or seven and I used to want you to just listen to me? I remember all the nice things you gave me for Christmas and my birthday and I was real happy with the things for about a week at the time I got the things, but the rest of the time during the year I really didn't want presents. I just wanted, all the time, for you to listen to me like I was somebody who FELT things, too, because I remember that even when I was so young, I felt things. But you said you were busy.

Mom, you are a wonderful cook and you have everything so clean and you were so tired so much from doing all those things that made you busy, but you know something, Mom? I would have liked crackers and peanut butter just as well—if you had only sat down with me a little while during the day and said to me, "Tell me all about it so I can maybe help you understand."

And when Donna came, I couldn't understand why everybody made so much fuss because I didn't think it was my fault that her hair is curly and her teeth are so white and she doesn't have to wear glasses with such thick lenses. Her grades were better, too, weren't they?

If Donna ever has any children, I hope you tell her to just pay some attention to the one that doesn't smile very much because that one will really be crying inside. And when she's about to bake six dozen cookies, to make sure first that the kids don't want to tell her about a dream or a hope or something because thoughts are important, too, to small kids even though they don't have so many words to use when they tell about what they have inside them.

I think that all the kids who are doing so many things that grownups are tearing their hair out worrying about, are really looking for somebody that will have time to listen a few minutes and who really and truly will treat them as they would a grownup who might be useful to them. You know—polite to them. If you folks had ever said to me: "Pardon me" when you interrupted me, I would have dropped dead!

If anybody asks you where I am, tell them I have gone looking for somebody with time, because I've got a lot of things I want to talk about.

Love to all,
Jerry[7]

Variations: Link or chain onto this example such other activities as these:

1. Ask, From a theological viewpoint, how much responsibility lies with Jerry, the writer of the letter?
2. Ask group members to share areas of personal concern which the case brought to mind.

Purpose: This activity should help learners interpret meanings and concepts.

Activity: Present a simple drawing which depicts an idea. Suggest that groups of two persons each develop a one-sentence interpretation.

Example: Ask the teacher trainees to study the following illustration for sixty seconds. Then ask: What does this drawing say about many of us as teachers? What do we need to do in this case?

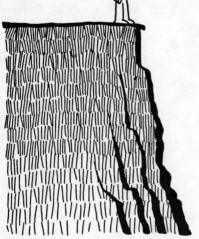

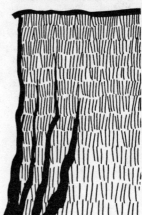

WHAT WE **KNOW** ABOUT HOW PERSONS LEARN

WHAT WE ACTUALLY DO IN THE CLASSROOM

Variations: Link or chain onto this example such other activities as these:

1. Ask learners to draw simple line drawings which depict (1) examples of teacher's doing the wrong things in the classroom and (2) teachers doing the right things. Call on several persons to share and explain their drawings.

2. Suggest that group members select the best and worst examples of teaching as suggested by the drawings. Ask them to arrange them on a bulletin board under the captions "do" and "don't."

49

Purpose: This activity should help the learner comprehend meanings. As a secondary value, it helps learners express ideas simply.

Activity: Ask learners to describe a concept or define a word using words of only one syllable.

ADULTS

Examples: 1. Ask the learners to define *sin* using no word of over one syllable. (One student defined the term this way: Sin means to say "I will do my own thing. God does not know how to run my life. I can run it. I do not need him.")
2. Ask students to rewrite the Preamble to the Constitution using no word of more than two syllables.

Variations: Link activities such as these onto the examples.
1. Ask the learners to define a word using a set number of words. For example: Define *sin*, but use no more than ten words.

YOUTH

2. Ask learners to define a term as if for an audience of children only.
3. Ask learners to define a term using as many words which begin with the same letter as possible.

Caution: Some persons may meet the syllable or word count requirement but miss the essence of the meaning.

Purpose: This activity should help learners develop analytical and problem-solving skills and use the elements of logic.

Activity: Present the learners with a series of steps in a process or a sequence of concepts. Ask them to produce a *graphic drawing* which depicts the relationships which exist between and among the parts.

Examples: 1. Draw a diagram which shows the relationship between rotation and revolution. (One learner produced the following.)

ADULTS

YOUTH

OLDER CHILDREN

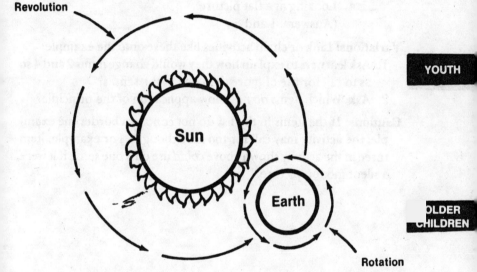

2. Draw a diagram which shows the relationship between conversion and salvation. (Conversion is a part of salvation—but the "front" or beginning part. Conversion is the beginning part of a continuing process called salvation.)

Variations: Link or chain onto the example such other activities as these:
1. Show a diagram first, then ask learners to determine from the diagram the relationships.
2. Draw parts of the diagram on separate pieces of cardboard. Ask learners to put the diagram together.

Purpose: This activity should help learners transfer learning to new situations.

Activity: Present visual or verbal illustrations in which a principle is or is not at work. Ask, Is the principle at work in this situation?

Example: Ask, Which of the following activities make use of the principle of multisensory perception (use of more than one of the senses) in teaching?

___ 1. Going on a trip
___ 2. Listening to an audiotape
___ 3. Viewing a motion picture
___ 4. Looking at a flat picture
      (Answers: 1 and 3.)

Variations: Link or chain activities like these onto the example:

1. Ask learners to explain how they would change items 2 and 4 so as to call for use of more than one of the senses?
2. Ask, Which items *do not* show application of the principle?

Cautions: If the items in the list do not contain a borderline example, the activity may call for too little thought. For example, item three in the activity shown above *could* use only one sense if it were a silent motion picture.

Purpose: This activity should help students formulate a principle.

Activity: Ask learners to formulate a principle after a demonstration or after reading a description of a process.

Example: Present to each pupil a two-inch square of cloth. Ask that they assume they must "test" the cloth before it leaves the factory. Ask, For what could we possibly test the cloth? (Colorfastness, durability, thread count, size, shrinkage, and so on.) Then ask: What would you use to test for these qualities? Would you test for colorfastness by rubbing the cloth with sandpaper or would you test it by exposing the cloth to a strong light bulb?

Ask, What principle can we derive from this illustration? (The test must suit the purpose. The test must reflect the objective.)

Variations: Link onto the example activities such these:

1. Display a yardstick, a piece of sandpaper, a magnifying glass, a light bulb, a glass of water, and so on. Ask, For what would you test this piece of cloth if your "tester" were one of these items? (Use a magnifying glass to test for thread count; a yardstick to test for size and so on.)
2. Write the following on a chalkboard. Then ask, Does the test match the objective? Why?

Objective	Test
The student will weave a basket	Explain the steps in weaving a basket.

(The test does not match the objective. The test should involve weaving a basket—not explaining how to weave a basket.)

Purpose: This activity should help learners develop problem-solving skills.

Activity: Display a picture (visual case study) which depicts a conflict in personal relationships. Ask learners to (1) identify the problem which they feel the case depicts, and (2) once they identify a problem to support with logical data the solution which they feel would best solve the problem.

Example: Display a picture such as the following. Ask, What problem(s) in family living do you feel exists? How would you handle the problem?

Variations: Link these attitudinal activities onto the example:
1. Change the learning outcome to the affective (attitudes and values) domain by asking such questions as these: Should fathers remain in the background when daughters and mothers have conflict? What differences in values do you feel might exist among the persons involved?
2. Lead learners to create a sentence story based on the picture. One person begins the story with one sentence; the second adds one sentence, and so on.

Cautions: Learners tend to read their own problems into the pictures. This could embarrass them if it becomes obvious or if other group members recognize that the problem actually exists in the life of the learner.

54

Purpose: This activity should help learners develop the ability to create new plans or ideas.

Activity: Present two approaches to the same process. Ask pupils to analyze the similarities and differences between them and to construct a plan of their own on the basis of the examples.

Example: Determine the similarities and differences between these two sets of steps in lesson planning. Then design a plan for lesson planning which reflects your own ideas.

No. 1	No. 2
Determine aims.	Determine goals and objectives.
Relate session to unit.	Design appropriate learning activities.
Select best methods.	Test.
Prepare learning aids.	
Plan for follow through.	
Evaluate results.	

Other possible subjects and materials: Plans for witnessing to others in church life; plans for Bible study; samples of personal data sheets to send to possible employers.

Variations: Link onto the examples activities such as these:
1. Ask learners to arrange the elements of lesson planning in what they consider the order of importance.
2. Ask learners to plan a lesson using their own plan for planning.
3. Ask learners to observe another teacher and discover the plan for planning he used.

Section II
Activities to Develop
Attitudes and Values

Purpose: This activity should help learners analyze their own values.

Activity: Present to the learners a short two- or three-sentence case study involving one's values. At the end of the case, ask, What should this person do?

Examples: 1. Write the following case on the chalkboard. "Peggy watches the principal search for the keys to his car, knowing that Dick has found them. Peggy has promised not to tell." Ask small study groups, What should Peggy do?
2. Read aloud this case: "Mary has a job cleaning out the supply room each week. She finds herself taking home larger and larger supplies of typing paper and carbon paper." Ask, How would you counsel Mary?

Variations: Link or chain onto these activities such other activities as these:
1. Lead the group in a Scripture search to determine guidelines for doing something about the situation.
2. Ask individuals to write a paragraph telling how they think Dick, Peggy, and the principal feel in the situation.

Purpose: This activity should help learners identify their own attitudes.

Activity: Show the learner a set of three or four pairs of pictures. In each pair, one picture shows a negative attitude about a person, place, or thing; the other shows the same situation but an opposite attitude. Ask learners to write a word or phrase, which tells which attitude each picture suggests.

Example:

"YOU NEVER COOK ANYTHING I LIKE!"

"I LIKE THE THINGS YOU COOK!"

Variations: Link onto this example such other activities as these:

1. Ask learners to recall and tell of times when they may have expressed the attitudes (both negative and positive) which the drawings depict.
2. Ask learners to find in magazines pictures which show persons demonstrating certain attitudes. (For example: unselfishness, selfishness, hatred, love, concern, joy, sharing, and so on.)

Purpose: This activity should help learners organize their values.

Activity: Ask learners to choose a nonhuman object which in some way reflects a personality trait they find desirable. Ask them to identify the object, the characteristic, and explain why they chose as they did.

Example: Ask each pupil to choose an animal whose basic characteristic suggests a desirable trait for persons to acquire. (For example, a child might choose a lion because of its strength and courage; a giraffe because it can "see things in perspective," and so on.) Then ask the pupils to tell why they chose and explain why.

Variations: Link onto this example such other activities as these:
1. Ask learners to choose an animal whose basic characteristic suggests an undesirable trait for persons to acquire. Ask them to name the trait and explain why they consider it undesirable.
2. Conduct a Scripture search in which learners find verses which describe characteristics of a Christian.

Purpose: This activity should help learners identify attitudes.

Activity: Ask the learner to express pictorially a set of given attitudes.

Example: Distribute to each learner a copy of the following line drawings. Include only the eyes on the faces. Ask the learner to draw the mouths so as to express such attitudes as these: anger, joy, sadness, surprise, rejection, haughtiness, empathy. (The first one is shown to make the idea clear.)

Variations: Link onto this example such other activities as these:
1. Ask the learners to complete a "face" expressing *their own* attitudes toward given persons, places, things. Ask, What attitudes *should* a Christian have in each case?
2. Complete the drawings yourself, then ask learners to match the faces with given attitudes.
3. Ask learners to draw the faces to reflect the attitudes of given Bible personalities as revealed in given passages of Scripture. For example, the father and the sons in the story of the prodigal son; the people in the parable of the good Samaritan.

Purpose: This activity should help learners value other persons.

Activity: Ask the learners to write a five-line poem about a person whom they value. Each line has a designated number of words and thoughts.

Example: Ask the learners to compose a five-line poem about the word *teacher*.

Use the following formula regarding number of words:

First line: one word, title

Second line: two words to explain

Third line: three words to tell what the title does

Fourth line: four words to tell how you feel about the title

Fifth line: one word that means the same as the title

One person wrote the following:

> Teacher
> My guide
> Helps me learn
> I love her so
> Friend

Variations: Link onto this example such other activities as these:

1. Substitute names of Bible personalities or literary characters for line one.
2. Ask learners to substitute names of friends or other persons who have influenced them in a positive way. Then ask learners to send the poems to the friend.

Purpose: This activity should help learners value the world of nature.

Activity: Ask the learners to compose a litany about things they value in the natural world. (A litany includes short phrases which identify things one values. Identical statements or responses follow each phrase.)

Example: Ask the learners, For what should we express thanks in the natural world? What things do you enjoy about the natural world? Who helps you each day? Write the responses on the chalkboard. Then lead the learners to express the ideas in litany form by adding "We thank you God" or some other meaningful sentence or phrase after each statement.

One group wrote this litany:

> For the grass so green
> WE THANK YOU GOD
> For the animals and birds
> WE THANK YOU GOD

Variations: Link onto this example such other activities as these:

1. Ask group members to read the litany responsively.
2. Ask learners to name a special friend and write down what they like about the friend. Then ask them to write a litany of gratitude for their friendship. The response line could read: "You are my friend."
3. Lead the learners to set the litany to music by using a hymn tune which fits the meter of the poem.

Purpose: This activity should help learners identify with the needs of others and adjust their attitudes and values.

Activity: Ask learners to write an original interpretation of a picture which portrays a situation with emotional content.

Example: Display the following illustration (a child in the midst of the rubble of war). Ask each learner to write a "thought narration" of the child's thoughts.

YOUTH

OLDER CHILDREN

Variations: Link activities like these onto the example:
1. Display such a picture, but ask learners to write a narrative about what could have been done *to prevent* such a situation. Call for reports.
2. Ask learners to collect from magazines pictures which illustrate the needs of the child.

Purpose: This activity should help learners understand what an attitude means.

Activity: Ask learners to depict through body movement or stance a given attitude.

Example: Ask several members of the group to arrange their hands to portray an assigned attitude. For example, to portray adoration, they could pose their hands to reverent prayer. Then ask other group members to name the attitude portrayed. Assign attitudes such as these, if appropriate to the lesson: concern, abandon, boredom, unconcern, compassion, worship or adoration, hatred.

Variations: Link onto this example such other activities as these:
1. Ask study groups of three or four each to portray a given attitude.
2. After a learner portrays a given attitude, ask her to pose so as to depict the opposite attitude. (For example: concern, unconcern; prejudice, respect for persons.)

Purpose: This activity should help learners develop values. (To establish priorities among several values.)

Activity: Ask learners to make one list of negative values or attitudes and a second list which includes only positive values or attitudes.

ADULTS

Example: Ask each learner to (1) list two words which he would like to have engraved on his tombstone and (2) two words which he would not like to appear on his tombstone. One person did it this way:

Do want:	*Do not want:*
Compassion	Gone!
Self-giving	Hurrah!

Then ask each person to explain why he or she chose each word.

Variations: Link onto this example such other activities as these:

YOUTH

1. Ask pupils to compile a list of words in each category and to arrange them in order of importance to them.
2. In the "tombstone" example, ask, If you had to remove one word in each list (leaving only one), which would you take out? Why?
3. Ask small groups of two or three to list ways in which persons reflect each value in real life.
4. Ask each person to think of one person who possesses one of the characteristics he would like to have on his tombstone. What, specifically, caused you to name him or her?
5. Ask each learner to describe the way he should live in order to avoid having a given word appear on his tombstone.

Cautions: Learners tend to write two-word phrases instead of two separate concepts. Either approach works, but two separate concepts call for more pupil activity.

Purpose: This activity should help learners listen to God's Word.

Activity: Ask learners to reflect on a given verse or passage from the Bible and identify a specific event in their own lives to which the verse speaks NOW.

Example: On the chalkboard, write "The Lord is my sheperd, I shall not want."

ADULTS

Ask learners to reflect in two or three minutes of silence on how the verse speaks to them presently. They should identify specific events. (For example: "I just got a letter this week telling me I had lost a contract I expected to get. But, regardless, God will take care of me.")

Variations: Link onto this example such other activities as these:
1. Ask individuals in groups of two or three to share what they thought about during the time of reflection.

YOUTH

2. Conduct a Scripture search for examples of Bible characters who found God faithful.

Purpose: This activity should help learners develop values.

Activity: Ask learners to assume that they are in a predicament in which they can take away with them only a few items. Ask, Which would you take?

ADULTS

Example: Ask each learner to assume that his house is on fire. Ask: In such a situation, which items would you try to take out with you if you had time to do so? Which would you take first? Why? What does your answer reveal about your value system?

Variations: 1. Assume that you have been given a "shopping spree" in a large department store. You know the location of all items. You have ten minutes in which to fill a shopping cart with items. Which items would you choose? Why?

YOUTH

2. Ask learners to assume the role of a specific other person (a national or world leader, a doctor, a teenager, a senior adult). Ask, what would each of them choose? Why?

Purpose: This activity should help learners organize their values.

Activity: Display a drawing which depicts a problem in juvenile delinquency. Then describe several persons of vastly different backgrounds who might have observed the problem. Ask learners to describe how each person, in the light of his or her background, might have interpreted or reacted to the problem.

ADULTS

Example: Display the drawings. Ask learners to describe how Mr. Hammond, Mrs. Granvil, and Mr. Grayson would have reacted to what they saw. Ask, Which values characterized each? Which reaction, in your opinion, would have been most redemptive? Why?

Variations: Link onto this example such other activities as these:

1. Present either the picture or a written case. Ask, With *which* of these three observers do you most readily identify? Why? In the light of your own sense of values, how do you feel you *should* respond?

YOUTH

2. Instead of a picture, read a case study which describes a problem related to values. Ask how given persons with vastly different backgrounds would likely respond.

MR. HAMMOND:

NEVER MARRIED; POLITICALLY LIBERAL; MEMBER TWO CIVIC SERVICE CLUBS; OWNS A CHAIN OF DRIVE-IN RESTAURANTS; GREW UP IN MIDDLE-CLASS FARM FAMILY; SIXTY YEARS OF AGE; ATTENDS CHURCH IRREGULARLY BUT HAS NEVER BEEN A MEMBER →

MRS. GRANVIL:

HAS NO CHILDREN; WIDOW; GREW UP IN UPPER-CLASS FAMILY; SPENDS WINTERS IN SUMMER HOME; SPONSORS AN INTERNATIONAL ART FESTIVAL; VOTES A CONSERVATIVE TICKET; FORTY-NINE YEARS OF AGE →

MR. GRAYSON:

GREW UP IN POVERTY; COMPLETED PH.D. IN ECONOMICS; HAS TWO TEEN-AGE SONS OF HIS OWN; SPONSORS A ROYAL AMBASSADORS' SOFTBALL TEAM; DOES VOLUNTEER SOCIAL WORK WITH A MISSION ACTION GROUP; THIRTY-FIVE YEARS OF AGE →

Purpose: This activity should help learners organize their values.

Activity: Present the learners with a list of desires or needs of persons. Ask the learners (1) to select those with which they identify most readily and (2) to arrange the needs or desires according to priority in their own lives.

Example: Distribute copies of the following prayer by Helmut Thielicke. Ask learners to circle the phrases with which they identify most. Then ask them to arrange in order of importance for them the three requests which follow "Heal us, O God, from . . ."

"O Lord, our God, we confess that often we do not like the bodies we have. Sometimes we have longed for jobs of others. We would like to do away with parts of our history. We are afraid of our moods and feelings. We wish we had more time. We would like to start over again. We lust after the prestige of others. We think more money will solve our problems. We resent the injustices we have suffered and cherish our sorrows. We want to be appreciated for our small graces. We are enchanted by the past and enticed by the future. We have never really been understood. In short, we have refused to live because we have held out for better terms. Heal us, O God, from the distance we have tried to put between ourselves and life. Restore to us the love of thee and all thy creation. Enable us by thy power to be renewed in our whole lives, through Jesus Christ our Lord. Amen."[8]

Variations: Link onto this example such other activities as these:
1. In advance, ask learners to list the complaints they sometimes have about life. Then present the prayer. Ask them to compare their list with Thielicke's.
2. Ask learners to classify the list of needs and desires according to the effect each would have on themselves, others, and God.

Purpose: This activity should help learners develop attitudes by reflecting on life's experiences.

Activity: Ask learners to chart or graph their growth or development in regard to some aspect of their emotional, intellectual, or spiritual lives.

Example: Ask learners to construct a line graph which depicts their ADULTS spiritual pilgrimage from conversion to the present. Then ask them to explain to another person what each point on the graph means. (For example, if the line comes near the bottom of the graph it might indicate a period of doubt. A high point on the graph could indicate a period in which the learner faced with faith a problem in life.)

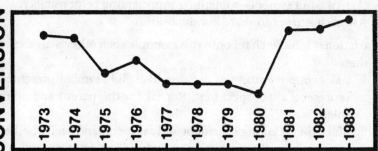

YOUTH

Variations: Link or chain onto this example such other activities as these:

1. Ask learners to recall the influence other persons had on them at various times in their lives. Or ask, What principles can you draw from the graph?
2. Ask learners to express their recollections in a form other than a line graph. (For example, one learner drew an ever-widening, upward spiral to indicate continuing growth.)
3. Ask learners to cut pictures from magazines and explain those which illustrate significant growth (or regression) experiences in their own lives.

Purpose: This activity should help learners develop their self-concept.

Activity: Ask the learner to select a "symbol" which she carries on her own person which represents her values or viewpoint toward persons, places, things.

ADULTS

Example: Some psychologists remind us that each of us is three persons—the parent, the adult, and the child. Ask each group member to find on her person (in a billfold, pocket, date book, and so on) the following:

(1) A child symbol—something light, entertaining.

(2) A parent symbol—something representing authority or other parental value.

(3) An adult symbol—something representing responsibility.

Ask each learner to share her discoveries.[9]

YOUTH

Variations: Link or chain onto this example such other activities as these:

1. Ask group members to decide which child symbol presented represents that aspect best. Repeat for the parent and adult role.

2. Make the following statement and ask members to tell whether they agree or disagree with it: An adult should put away all evidences of the child in his personality.

Purpose: This activity should help learners develop a sense of values toward the natural world.

Activity: Ask learners to go through the act of "destroying" a bit of nature, then challenge them to put it together again as it was before.

Example: Obtain some soil from a place where it would likely contain different kinds of grasses and other plants and several items, such as cigarette butts, plastic, and other refuse. Place it on a table under a cloth. Remove the cloth. Ask members to use knives and forks to tear the dirt apart. Ask them to find as many different kinds of plants, roots, seeds, leaves, and "garbage" items as possible. Ask, What does your analysis say about God's creation? (It is marvelous in variety. Humans are encroaching on it with refuse, etc.)

ADULTS

Variations: Link onto this example such other activities as these:

1. Ask learners to attempt to put it together again—just as it was. Ask, How do you feel as you try to put it together again? (Probably guilty.)

YOUTH

2. Ask each learner to list ways in which he or she upsets or destroys God's creation without need and to make a list of what he or she can do to change such actions.

Purpose: This activity should help learners respond creatively to the appeals made by media.

Activity: Ask learners to analyze the appeals made by certain aspects of the media, to evaluate the appeals, and to respond objectively.

Example: Ask learners to bring to class a daily newspaper. Ask them to analyze the appeal each advertisement makes. (For example: appeals to ego, spiritual need, impulse, sex, appetite, vanity, love of money, and so on.) Then ask them to rate the advertisements in regard to the extent to which the learner *needs* the actual item advertised and the extent to which the ad seems to manipulate the reader.

ADULTS

Variations: Link onto this example such other activities as these:

1. Ask learners to find Bible verses which reflect on the appeals contained in the ads. In what order would a Christian rank the appeals? Non-Christian? In what order do *you* rank them according to your own standards?

YOUTH

2. Ask selected learners to write several TV commercials (or watch them in the group) and make the same analysis. Ask, What aspects of an advertising appeal can television carry which print cannot carry? (Tone of voice, etc.)

Purpose: This activity should lead learners to reflect upon their system of values.

Activity: Provide a list of several pairs of personal traits. Each pair includes the positive trait and its opposite, such as stingy, generous. Ask learners to circle the three words which they would most and least like to characterize them.

ADULTS

Example: Provide each learner with the following sets of personal traits:

foolish—wise	quick—slow
careful—careless	tidy—untidy
truthful—untruthful	dishonest—honest
stingy—generous	kind—unkind
lazy—industrious	dirty—clean

Variations: Link onto this example such other activities as these:

YOUTH

1. Ask learners to tell of a time when they did something which showed a negative trait (stingy, careless, so on.)
2. Ask learners to tell of someone they know who has one of the positive traits. Ask them to tell what the person *did* which showed he was careful, honest, kind, and so on.
3. Ask learners to tell what they could do to show kindness instead of unkindness and so on.

Purpose: This activity should help learners develop a system of values.

Activity: Ask learners to write a narrative describing the feelings of a person who has just been delivered from an accident or other kind of catastrophe.

ADULTS

Examples: 1. Ask a pupil to read aloud Mark 5:22-24, 35-42. Then ask the pupils to answer in writing the following question: What if the little girl Christ raised from the dead had kept a diary? What would she have written in it? Ask learners to share their compositions with the group.

2. Ask learners to study the "sheep and shepherd" passages in the New Testament and write a one day's diary about what happened in the life of Mr. A. Shepherd.

YOUTH

Variations: Link onto this example such other activities as these:
1. Ask learners to write in dialogue form instead of diary form.
2. Ask learners to write several diary entries from their own diaries. Ask, What does this say about what you value most?

76

Purpose: This activity should help learners value other persons.

Activity: Ask learners to think of a given inanimate object as representing a person they love. On signal, ask the learners to do something destructive to the object. Some will not do it; others will, just to follow instructions. Lead both groups to analyze their feelings abouth the destructive action.

ADULTS

Example: Provide each learner with an 8½-by-11-inch sheet of paper. Ask learners to look at the paper, hold it in front of them, and imagine that it represents the person who means more to them than any other. Suggest that they recall how the person looks. Ask them to recall *why* they feel as they do about the person. With a sheet of paper in your own hand, ask the members of the group to do with the paper what you do. Then suddenly crumple the paper and throw it on the floor. (Some will hesitate; others will not do it; others will.) Then ask questions like these: Why did some of you refuse to crumple the paper? What happens to another person when you "crumple" him or her by your actions? Do you value the other person more or less after this activity? Why?

YOUTH

Variations: Link onto this activity such other activities as these:
1. Ask those who crumpled the paper to attempt to smooth it out, just as it was. Then ask, What does this say to you about the times you have hurt or otherwise "crumpled" a person?
2. Reverse the activity by asking them to think of a person who wronged them at some time. Then lead a discussion of their feelings.

Caution: Because of the emotional nature of the activity, don't be alarmed at the shedding of tears.

Purpose: This activity should help learners identify attitudes and understand what they mean.

Activity: Provide for the learners a crossword puzzle which uses attitudinal words such as *love, hate, prejudice, acceptance, concern.*

Example: Give to each learner a copy of the crossword puzzle. Then ask such questions as: Which words have synonyms in the puzzle? Tell of a time when you experienced one of these attitudes. What should you do about a negative attitude?

Variations: Link onto this example such other activities as these:

1. Ask learners to identify a Bible personality or literary character who possessed the attitude.
2. Ask learners to create a puzzle themselves.
3. Ask learners to create a puzzle which uses attitudinal words and their opposites.

Answers:

Down	Across
1. hostility	4. cool
2. antagonism	5. angry
3. mad	6. sad
	7. discord

Down

1. H_____ is an angry, unfriend-ly, feeling.
2. A_____ is what you feel when you oppose something or when two people have conflict.
3. I'm M_____ at you! You might say to someone who ate your hot fudge sundae.

Across

4. You might be C_____ to someone who likes to fight.
5. We say we feel mad or A_____.
6. If you get mad at someone, you may later feel S_____.
7. When there is disagreement, there is D_____.

Purpose: This activity should help learners organize their values.

Activity: Ask the learner to assume that an emergency confronts him. He needs to flee but has time to take with him only two or three things. Ask, What would you take?

ADULTS

Example: Ask the learner to assume that he is in a library. He is about to leave for a destination which has no libraries. He can only take three books. Ask, Which three books would you take? Why?

Variations: Link or chain onto this example such other activities as these:

1. Ask the learner to assume he found his house burning. Time permits the rescue of only a few things. Ask, Which things would you take out first, second, and so on? Why?

YOUTH

2. Ask the learner to assume that refugees from political persecution surround him. He has twelve hours to do whatever he chooses to help them. Ask, What would you do first? Second? Why?

3. Ask the learner to choose from a billfold or purse the two things he would keep if he had to choose. Ask, Why did you choose those things?

(Apply the activity to other life situations—leisuretime activities, church activities, civic activities, and so on.)

Purpose: This activity should help learners value other persons and develop concern for them.

Activity: Ask learners to take a positive action toward a person in need.

Example: Ask learners to bring to the session a copy of the daily newspaper. Ask them to find in the paper a story or report of someone who has faced a tragedy such as loss of a loved one or loss of possessions in a fire. Ask learners to write a letter of sympathy or encouragement to the persons involved.

ADULTS

Variations: Link onto this example such other activities as these:
1. Ask learners to mail the letters and share replies later.
2. Ask members in groups of two to tell each other about a personal need and to explain what they would most like others to do (or not to do) in response.

YOUTH

Purpose: This activity should help learners value other persons.

Activity: Lead learners in a mock-up situation to reflect on the feelings of (1) a person excluded from a group and (2) group members who have excluded a person.

Example: On the chalkboard, draw an illustration similar to the following:

ADULTS

YOUTH

Divide group members into two groups of equal size. Ask group 1 to focus attention on the excluded one and (1) list several questions the excluded one is probably asking himself and (2) write a short paragraph describing the feelings of the one left out.

Ask group 2 to focus attention on the other group members. Ask them to (1) list several "reasons" why they may have excluded the person and (2) write a short paragraph describing their feelings toward one another and toward the excluded one.

Variations: Link to this activity such other activities as these:
1. Assume that the excluded one feels left out because of a birth defect, lack of education, or a difference in doctrinal conviction. Ask, How would you feel in such a case? What should group members do to bring the person within the circle?
2. Assume that the group had appointed a group member to approach the "outsider" to invite him or her to become part of the group. Ask two members to role-play the conversation.

Purpose: This activity should help learners organize their values.

Activity: Ask learners to compare the motives of the promises they make to God with the promises they make to others.

Example: On the chalkboard, make two columns headed "Promises We Make to God" and "Promises We Make to Others." Ask learners to list motives for promises in the first column (to change lives, to help others, to grow spiritually). Then ask them to list the motives for promises in the second column (to gain money, popularity, to make one's self comfortable).

ADULTS

Variations: Link onto this example such other activities as these:

1. Ask, Is it true that, when we promise something to another person, we at the same time promise it to God? Ask small study groups to discuss the question and present answers.
2. Lead the group in a Scripture search on the role of God's promises in the Christian life.

YOUTH

Purpose: This activity should help learners value the uniqueness of their bodies.

Activity: Ask the learner to perform some function without using some essential bodily capability.

Example: Provide each learner with a large sheet of paper and pencils in several colors. *Blindfold the learners.* Ask them to draw a vase of flowers or some other simple object, using the colored pencils. Display the drawings. Then discuss questions like these: What mistakes does vision help us avoid?

Variations: Link onto this example such other activities as these:

1. Devise experiments in which pupils cannot use the other senses or bodily capabilities. (For example, open a door without use of hands.)

2. Ask volunteers to do an experiment in which they extend the "blindfolded" time to one hour. Ask them to report later, describing their feelings and difficulties.
3. Ask, If you had to do without one of your five senses, which would you leave out? Why?

Purpose: This activity should help learners organize their own value systems.

Activity: Ask learners to suggest the name of a person whom they feel would fill creatively a given role in life's relationships.

Examples: 1. Ask learners to consider whom they would choose for parents if they had no parents. Then ask them to explain why they chose those persons.

ADULTS

2. Ask learners: If you could choose only one teacher who would teach you for a lifetime, who would that teacher be? Describe her or him. What characteristics does this person have?

Variations: Link onto this example such other activities as these:

1. Ask learners to arrange the characteristics of that person in order of importance.

2. Ask learners to name a popular personality whom they *would not like* to fill that particular role. (You may want to

YOUTH

avoid names and ask the learners to say simply, "I'm thinking of a person who has these characteristics which I do not want to have . . .)

3. Ask pupils to "create" a composite person by saying "I want parents who are honest as Abraham Lincoln, as loving as ___, as funny as ___, as wise as ___, . . ."

Purpose: This activity should help learners clarify their self-concept.

Activity: Ask the learner to choose from a collection of nonpersonal objects or pictures the one which she feels "resembles" her best. Ask her to explain why she chose the object.

Example: On separate sheets of paper fasten pictures of various kinds of cars, trucks, and buses. Place one picture on each piece. Choose vehicles which differ widely in style, purpose, and so on. Ask each learner to study the pictures and decide which one "resembles" her most. Ask her to tell why she chose that particular picture.

Variations: Link to this example such other activities as these:
1. Ask group members to describe the kind of car they think other persons in the group would drive, given a choice. (Or they may describe the kind of house they think the person would like to live in.)
2. Ask individual members to stand before the group as other members call out good points they have observed in him or her. (For example: trustworthy, thoughtful, etc.)

Caution: In the variation where learners describe a given person, feelings could easily be hurt. Know the group before using this variation.

Purpose: This activity should help learners value personal growth.

Activity: Provide a scheme whereby learners identify significant spiritual events in their lives. Ask them to explain what happened.

Example: Place in front of the class a large map of the United States. Give each learner several blank paper flags and straight pins. Ask them to write their names on the flags and place them on the map at places where significant events in their spiritual lives took place. Then ask each person to explain the event.[9]

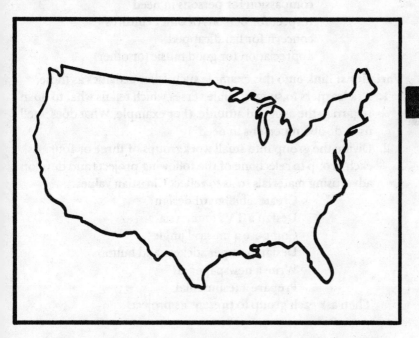

Variations: Link or chain to this example such activities as these:
1. Ask learners to name persons who influenced them in regard to the spiritual event and tell what they did.
2. Ask learners to mail thank-you letters to persons who have influenced them.

Purpose: This activity should help learners organize their values.

Activity: Lead the group to select a desirable attitudinal characteristic (concern, helpfulness, compassion, respect, etc.). Make assignments to small groups to develop an assigned part of an advertising campaign to "sell" the attitude.

ADULTS

Example: On the chalkboard, write the following list of attitudes. Ask learners to select one for which to develop an advertising campaign.

> compassion for persons in need
> respect for persons of other cultures
> concern for handicapped
> appreciation for good music (or other)

Variations: Link onto this example such other activities as these:

YOUTH

1. Ask learners to suggest Bible verses which tell us what to do in regard to the assigned attitude. (For example, What does it tell us to do about persons in need?)
2. Divide the group into small workgroups of three or four. Ask each group to select one of the following projects and develop advertising materials so as to reflect Christian values.

> Create a billboard design
> Design a TV commercial
> Compose a musical jingle
> Design bumper stickers and buttons
> Write a newspaper ad
> Prepare a testimonial

Then ask each group to present its project.

88

Purpose: This activity should help learners develop their self-concept.

Activity: Ask learners to choose from a list of positive personality traits those which they feel they possess.

Example: Ask group members to study the following list of personality traits (or a similar list). Then ask them to select the three traits which they feel best describe them.

ADULTS

trustworthy	prompt
sincere	consistent
helpful	respectful
energetic	thoughtful
patient	open-minded
caring	happy

After they select the words, ask them to tell an incident in their lives where they showed the characteristic.

YOUTH

Variations: Link onto this example such other activities as the following:

1. Ask, How did you feel when you told another person about your good points? Hesitant? Embarrassed? Why?
2. Into the list of characteristics insert several which one could think of as either positive or negative, depending on the situation. For example: aggressive, ambitious. Ask for examples of negative and positive aspects of aggressiveness, ambition, and so on.

Purpose: This activity should help learners value individual differences.

Activity: Contrive a situation in which learners must depend on other persons to accomplish a task.

Example: Arrange the room to provide a large open space in the center. Group members may sit around the walls. Ask for four volunteers. Select one strong heavyweight and three who do not weigh much. Tell the four that they constitute one body. The strongest person is the group's feet; another, the arms; another, the eyes; another, the mouth.

Place an object on the opposite side of the room from the four. A life preserver (such as provided on a ship for emergencies) would add a sense of urgency to the activity. Ask that the four

work together to take the life preserver to another designated person in the group. Then ask, What feelings did you have during the activity? What temptations did you have (such as temptation to do the other person's job)? If one person had done the work assigned to another, how would the second person have felt?

Variations: Link onto this example such other activities as these:
1. Divide the group into groups of four. Ask each person to tell the others what he himself can do best in situations which call for group cooperation. Then ask each person to tell each of the others what he feels *they* do well in group activity.
2. Ask, What understanding about the church does this activity suggest?

Cautions: Some learners may hesitate to talk about what they themselves do well. They may feel it sounds egotistical. Assure them that it is not.

Purpose: This activity should help learners develop their system of values.

Activity: Lead the learners to determine in a systematic way the relative time value given to certain activities.

Example: Distribute to each learner a copy of the following "time inventory sheet." Ask learners to keep a one-day record, by fifteen-minute intervals of how they spend their time. A record of Monday through Sunday would provide a more accurate record. Ask them to total the time by hours and list the categories in the order of amount of time spent.

| TIME | | ACTIVITY DESCRIPTION |
Began	Time Spent	(What, why, how many, etc.)

Variations: Link onto this example such other activities as these:

1. Ask learners to write a letter of resolve, to themselves, listing changes they want to make, based on findings from their time chart.

2. Ask them to make a list of ways they *should* spend their time, along with an estimated time desired. Then ask, What revisions do you need to make in order to improve your time schedule? What do you need to eliminate? Add?

Purpose: This activity should help learners develop their self-concept.

Activity: Ask the learners to rate themselves on several traits and roles.

Example: Distribute to each learner a copy of the following chart:

	1	2	3	4	5	6
Leadership ability	__	__	__	__	__	__
Ability to relate creatively to others	__	__	__	__	__	__
Diligence	__	__	__	__	__	__
Honesty	__	__	__	__	__	__
Ability to listen	__	__	__	__	__	__
Generosity	__	__	__	__	__	__
Trustworthiness	__	__	__	__	__	__
Ability to make and keep friends	__	__	__	__	__	__

Direct them to make a graph showing the points which best show their self-concept in that particular area. Number 6 means a high rating; number 1 a low rating. They may check the places with lead pencils.

Variations: Link or chain onto this example such other activities as these:

1. If the learners are mature enough to "risk" finding out what others think, ask members in groups of two to rate *each other* and compare what others think with what one thinks of himself.

2. Write on the chalkboard the names of such Bible personalities as Moses, Jacob, Abraham, Paul, and Judas. Ask learners to use the graph to rate the characters.

Purpose: This activity should help learners organize their system of values.

Activity: Present a list of four to six concerns which learners may have. Ask them to rank them in order of importance and explain why.

Example: On the chalkboard, write the following human needs:

ADULTS

> Family needs
> Educational needs
> Spiritual needs
> Financial needs
> Health needs

Ask learners in two or three minutes of silence to rank the needs in order of importance to them. After individual reports, ask, Why did you arrange the items in that order?

YOUTH

Variations: Link or chain onto this example such other activities as these:

1. Write the needs on cardboard placards. Ask learners to select one which they feel could serve as an umbrella under which all the others could fit. Arrange the placards on the floor or on a cling chart.
2. Write the needs as headings across the chalkboard. Ask learners to conduct a Scripture search to locate verses which indicate that individuals have responsibilities in each area.

Section III
Activities to Develop
Memory—Recall Abilities

Purpose: This activity should help learners recall facts and information.

Activity: Ask learners to seal in a container for later opening the significant facts and ideas in a unit of study. At a predetermined time in the future, ask the learners to open the container and read its contents for review purposes.

Example: Show the learners a long, slender olive jar (or similar glass container) to serve as a "time capsule." Ask each member of the group to write on paper one or two significant facts about a unit of study just completed. Ask them to place the papers in the jar, seal it, and place it out of sight in the room. On the top write "Don't open until __(date)__ .

On that date, ask a student to open the "time capsule" and distribute the papers to students who will read the facts aloud.
Use facts like these:

   The Dead Sea has lower elevation than the Sea of Galilee.
   Palestine had five political subdivisions.
   Nazareth is east of the Sea of Galilee.
   Jericho has a lower elevation than Jerusalem.

Variations: Link onto this example such other activities as these:
   1. Insert questions instead of facts into the time capsule. Include enough to provide a good test on the unit. Ask learners to write the questions themselves. Eliminate duplicates.
   2. Ask learners to write short newspaper articles (one paragraph) about the unit. Insert them in the capsule and ask pupils to read them at a later date.

Purpose: This activity should help learners recall or recognize facts and information.

Activity: "Hide" short words in longer words. Ask the learner to find the hidden words. Use words related to the subject studied.

Example: Circle the little word in the big word.

each	—— in ——	preacher
know	—— in ——	knowledge
love	—— in ——	unloved
give	—— in ——	forgive
ark	—— in ——	darkness

Variations: Link or chain onto this example such other activities as these:

1. Ask learners to make a list of words in a given story. Then ask them to think of larger words in which the small word appears. In this way, they make their own activity to share with others in the group.
2. Cut words into sections by syllables. Ask learners to create as many new words as they can think of.
3. Write on the chalkboard a syllable from a word. Ask learners to think of other words which contain that syllable.

Purpose: This activity should help learners recall facts and information.

Activity: "Hide" information in the body of a narrative. Ask learners to find the information and underline it.

Example: Present the learners with a copy of the following narrative. Ask them to underline the names of twenty books of the Bible hidden in the material.

I once made some re<u>marks</u> about hidden books of the Bible. It was a lu<u>lu</u>! <u>Kept</u> some people loo<u>king so</u> hard for <u>facts</u> and studying for <u>revelation</u>! They were in a <u>jam</u>—especially since the books were not capitalized, but the <u>truth</u> finally struck <u>numbers</u> of our readers. To others it was a hard <u>job</u>. We want it to be <u>a most</u> fascinating few moments for you. <u>Yes, there</u> will be some real easy to spot; others may require <u>judges</u> to determine. We must admit <u>it usually</u> takes a minute to find one, and there will be loud <u>lamentations</u> when you see how simple it was. One "Jane" says <u>she brews</u> her coffee while she puzzles her brain. Another "<u>Joe</u>" looks for a gimmick. Ah, but it can be done by an old <u>hag! Gain</u> may come slowly, but it's as easy as peeling a banana. <u>Hum</u> a tune while you rack your brain with this <u>chronicle</u>. Happy Hunting![1]

Variations: Link onto the example such other activities as these:
1. Ask learners to classify the books according to New or Old Testament, and to list them in order.
2. Ask learners to compose their own story so as to include names of other books of the Bible.

YOUTH

OLDER
CHILDREN

Purpose: This activity should help learners recall facts and information.

Activity: Present to the students a list of key words in a Bible verse, a statement of a principle, or a famous quotation. Ask them to reconstruct the complete statement.

Example: On the chalkboard, write the following words.

others	things	also
heard	commit	men
witnesses	teach	

Ask learners to reconstruct the original statement. "And the things thou hast heard of me among many witnesses, the same commit thou to faithful men who shall be able to teach others also" (2 Tim. 2:2).

Variations: Link onto the example such other activities as these:

1. Play a recall game by writing only one word on the chalkboard at a time. Keep adding words until each learner has determined the entire statement.
2. Ask learners, in groups of two, to say to each other, "I am thinking of a Bible verse which contains the word *witnesses.* The person keeps providing words until the other group member recalls the verse.
3. Write the key words on 3 by 5 cards. Ask learners to arrange them in the order in which they would appear in a Bible verse.

Purpose: This activity should help learners recall facts and information.

Activity: Present to the learners a picture of an actual event from a given story. Ask them to recall the events which preceded and followed.

Example: Ask what things happened before and after this picture?

SAMUEL SAMUEL

GOD CALLS TO SAMUEL

Variations: Link to the example such activities as these:
1. Ask children to draw pictures of the events which preceded and followed the event shown in the example.
2. Ask children to *pose* events in a story.

Purpose: This activity should help learners recall facts and information.

Activity: Ask learners to tell a composite or round-robin story. Each learner in turn adds one sentence to the story.

Example: Display a Bible picture of Naomi and Ruth. Ask one learner to begin the Bible story by saying something like "Naomi and her family lived in Bethlehem." Ask each of the other group members to add one sentence to the story. Continue until they present the essential parts of the story.

For example: Naomi and her family lived in Bethlehem.
Naomi's husband's name was Elimelech.
They migrated from Bethlehem to Moab.
Naomi's husband died after they arrived in Moab.
Her two sons married Moabite women, Orpah and Ruth.

YOUTH

After ten years her sons died, leaving Orpah and Ruth as widows.
And so on.

Variations: Link or chain onto this example such other activities as these:

1. Show a scrambled list of facts in the story. Ask learners to arrange them in chronological order.
2. After completing the story, ask groups of two or three to write

OLDER CHILDREN

five adjectives each which describe Naomi and Ruth. Call for reports.

Caution: See that group members study the story carefully in advance.

Purpose: This activity should help learners recall facts and information.

Activity: Cut a picture or a map into small squares. Ask learners to identify an object or location based only on information contained in the square.

Example: Cut into small squares a map of the United States. (Use longitude and latitude markers as guides.) Distribute the squares at random. Ask students to answer such questions as these regarding the segment:
1. Does it belong east or west of the Mississippi?
2. In which state does it belong?
3. Using a map legend, what altitude does it suggest?
4. Does it belong north or south of the Mason-Dixon line?

YOUTH

Variations: Link onto this example such other activities as these:
1. Include in the set of squares one which *does not belong.* After the students discover that it does not belong, ask, How do you *know* it belongs somewhere else? *Where* does it belong?
2. Instead of a map, use a detailed drawing of a sailing vessel, an automobile engine, or other items which require knowledge of detail.

Cautions: Use of large squares lessens the challenge of the activity. Learners should have to recall significant details.

CHILDREN

Purpose: This activity should help learners recall facts and information.

Activity: Write on the chalkboard a sentence, phrase, or a Bible verse for memorization. Using the fading technique, erase one at a time the important words (nouns, verbs, adjectives, etc.). Call on a learner to read the statement aloud, supplying the missing word or words. Then begin to erase the more unimportant words (prepositions, definite articles, etc.) and continue the plan. Continue until only one unimportant word remains.

Example: On the chalkboard, write: "For by grace are ye saved through faith; and that not of yourselves; it is the gift of God" (Eph. 2:8). Then in steps like the following, "fade" the verse so that the learner must supply more and more himself.

"For by grace are ye _____ through _____; and that not of yourselves; it is the gift of God."

YOUTH

"For by grace are ye _____ through _____; and that not of yourselves; it is the _____ of God."

"For by _____ are ye _____ through _____; and that not of _____ it is the _____ of God."

"For by _____ __ ye _____ _____ _____; and that not of _____ it is the _____ of _____."

"_____ _____ _____ __ __ _____ _____ _____; and _____ _____ __ _____ it _____ __ _____ __ _____."

Variations: Link or chain onto this example such other activities as these:

1. Ask students to recite the verse, but to insert synonyms for the important words. In this way the learning level rises to comprehension.

CHILDREN

2. Write the words on separate cardboard strips or 3 by 5 cards. Ask learners to arrange them so as to form the quotation.

101

Purpose: This activity should help learners recall facts and information and develop vocabulary.

Activity: Ask learners to find as many words as possible in a given word.

Example: On the chalkboard write the word *immediately.* Ask learners to write as many words as they can find in the one word. Then call from reports from all learners. List the words on the chalkboard.

One group found these words:

yield	met	tale	dam
mediate	date	mail	dim
tame	mate	meet	immediate
yet	dial	yam	team

YOUTH

Variations: Link onto this example such other activities as these:

1. Ask learners to write as many words of four or more letters as possible.
2. Ask learners to write as many words as possible beginning with the letter *m, d,* and so on.
3. Ask them to write only nouns, verbs, or adjectives.
4. Assign a rating system such as: thirty words, excellent; twenty-four words, good; eighteen words, fair. The number will depend on the original word.

CHILDREN

Purpose: This activity should help learners recall facts and information.

Activity: Show pictures of persons or events. Ask learners to identify the events or persons.

Example: Study the pictures. Under each picture, write the event in Baptist history which it depicts.

1. _____

1. _____

Drawings from *Baptist Adults*, April-June, 1964. © Copyright 1964, The Sunday School Board of the Southern Baptist Convention. Used by permission.

Variations: Link or chain onto this example such other activities as these:

1. Ask learners to arrange the events in chronological order.
2. Provide a list of dates. Ask learners to match the dates with the pictures of events.

Purpose: This activity should help learners recall facts and information.

Activity: Cut several maps into one- or two-inch squares. (Road maps, for example.) Shuffle the squares. Then ask learners to identify individual squares as to state, nation, and so on.

Example: Cut a map of Palestine into one- or two-inch squares. (Use a map approximately 9 by 12 if you choose one-inch squares.) Distribute squares to individual students. Ask them to identify rivers, lakes, the divisions of the country, and so on.

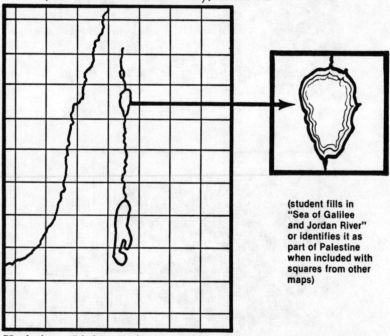

(student fills in "Sea of Galilee and Jordan River" or identifies it as part of Palestine when included with squares from other maps)

Variations: Link onto the example such other activities as these:

1. Print several map segments on a sheet of paper as an "identification exercise." Reproduce several of the map squares in random order on a sheet of paper. Ask students to determine the state or country to which it belongs.

2. Distribute several squares to each student. Ask students to trade until they accumulate all the squares for their particular map. They should complete the map of which their first square is a part.

104

Purpose: This activity should help learners recall facts and information.

Activity: Arrange for learners to receive a stimulus word, phrase, or concept which requires a response or a translation. Ask them to respond, then give immediate knowledge of results.

Example: On 3 by 5 cards write the letters of the Hebrew alphabet. On the other side write the English equivalent. Flash the cards to the learners and ask for their translation. To give immediate knowledge of results, display the other side of the card after they respond.

ADULTS

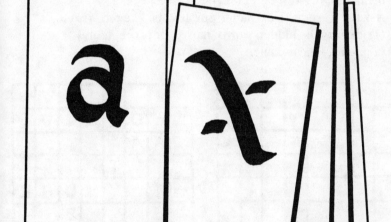

YOUTH

Variations: Link onto the example activities such as these:
1. Organize the group as in a spelling bee. Display the flash cards to the first person in line, one at a time. If she responds correctly she stays in line; if not, she sits down. Continue until one side wins—by having the greatest number of persons standing at the end of the activity.

CHILDREN

2. Conduct the activity as a round robin. After one person answers correctly, she may call on another person of her choosing to respond to the next one. Continue until all cards have been used at least once.

Purpose: This activity should help learners recall facts and information.

Activity: Ask learners to prepare their own hidden word puzzle related to a unit of study. Then ask them to exchange puzzles with other persons who will try to discover the hidden words.

Example: Provide each person with a copy of a grid similar to the illustration. (Ten rows of ten squares is adequate, but use more if you desire.) Ask each learner to study one of the parables and select five to ten words, names, or concepts which the parable represents. Then ask him to write the words forwards, backwards, up and down, or diagonally on the grid. He should then fill in the blank squares with other letters.

Ask the learners to exchange puzzles. Ask the recipient to
(1) identify the hidden words, names, or concepts and
(2) identify the parable.

YOUTH

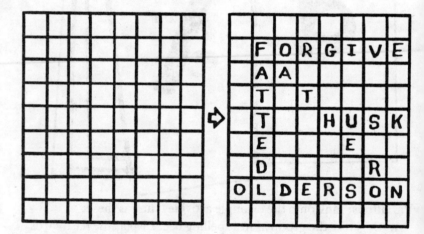

Variations: Link or chain onto this example such other activities as these:

1. After learners complete the puzzles, ask each to call out the hidden words while other learners identify the parable.
2. Write on 3 by 5 cards the words from several parables. Scramble the cards. Ask learners to determine which parables the words represent.

Purpose: This activity should help learners recall facts and information.

Activity: Display in random order a set of words which depict parts of a sequence of events or processes. Ask learners to arrange them in a predetermined order (logical, chronological, alphabetical, and so on).

ADULTS

Example: Arrange in order the following events in the story of redemption in the Bible:

      __ 1. baptism of John
      __ 2. resurrection of Jesus
      __ 3. man's fall
      __ 4. creation of man
      __ 5. birth of Jesus
      __ 6. crucifixion
      __ 7. burial of Jesus
      __ 8. Jesus' ministry in Judea
      __ 9. the Last Supper
      __10. ascension

YOUTH

Variations: Link to this example such other activities as these:

1. Ask one student to do the arranging while other students tell him or her where to place the items.
2. Arrange the items in order except for two items. Ask, Which items break the order? Where do they belong?
3. Distribute the word strips to group members. Ask them to hold the word strip in front of them and to arrange themselves in the right order as others instruct them.

OLDER CHILDREN

Purpose: This activity should help learners recall facts.

Activity: Label the walls of a classroom to represent north, south, east, and west. Ask learners to stand in the place where they would find certain geographical features if the room were a map. Write the names of political subdivisions (counties, etc.), rivers, mountains, and other geographical data on cardboard strips large enough for the entire class to see. Distribute strips to the students.

Ask the students who hold assigned cards to walk to the section of the room where the geographical point is located. Those who have names of rivers will "run" or "walk" the length of the river to show the location. (Or they could stretch a length of blue ribbon to show its location.)

Example: See illustration, page 109.

Variations: Link onto the example such activities as these:
1. Substitute products (cotton, oil, iron ore, automobiles, etc.) for places. Ask students to stand where the particular product is produced.
2. Ask students to "walk" certain journeys. For example, "Walk the route Cortez took from Vera Cruz to Mexico City when he conquered Mexico."
3. Write the locations (or products) on placards. Place them at *incorrect* locations about the room. Ask students to rearrange the room so that placards stand in correct places.

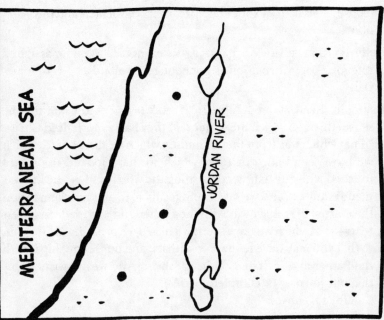

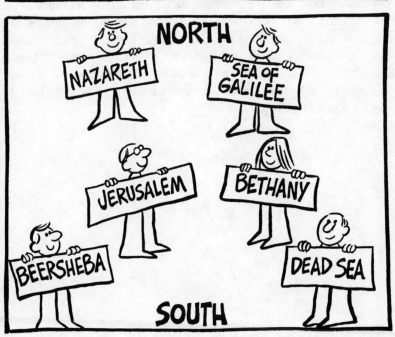

Purpose: This activity should help learners recall facts and information.

Activity: As an advance organizer, ask learners to listen for assigned categories of information as someone reads aloud a body of material.

ADULTS

Example: Read aloud 1 John 1:1-4. Ask learners to listen for the senses through which the writer said they had experienced Christ. "That which was from the beginning, which we have heard, which we have seen with our eyes, which we have looked upon and touched with our hands, concerning the word of life—the life was made manifest, and we saw it, and testify to it, and proclaim to you the eternal life which was with the Father and was made manifest to us—that which we have seen and heard we proclaim also to you, so that you may have fellowship with us; and our fellowship is with the Father and with his Son Jesus Christ. And we are writing this that our joy may be complete" (RSV).

YOUTH

Call for responses.

Variations: Link onto this example such other activities as these:
1. Provide a Bible commentary. Ask learners to interpret what the writer had in mind by saying "seen," "heard," and "touched." (This raises the learning level to comprehension.)
2. On the chalkboard, write these captions: sight, hearing, touch. Ask learners to suggest ways in which we see, hear, and touch in spreading the gospel.

Purpose: This activity should help learners recall facts and information.

Activity: Ask learners to visually relate events to the place where they happened.

Example: Ask learners to clip news items from the daily newspaper. Then ask them to prepare a bulletin board on which they connect with string the dateline (which gives the location) with the place on the map where the event happened.

ADULTS

YOUTH

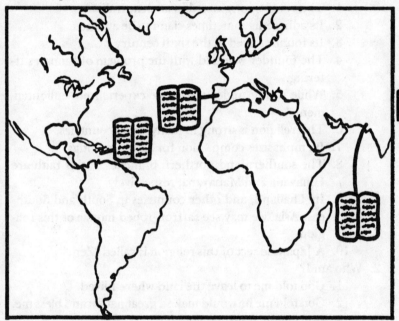

Variations: Link to this example such other activities as these:
1. Ask learners to figure the percentage of world news to local news as represented by the clippings.
2. Instead of posting items, ask learners to read a news item and request another learner to find it on the map.

Purpose: This activity should help learners recall facts and information.

Activity: Present to the learner, in random order, a list of clues to identify a person, place, or idea. Ask the learner to discover the answer using as few of the facts as possible.

Examples: 1. The following facts serve as clues to the identification of a world religion. Begin with the first one. How far down the list do you have to go before identifying the religion?

1. This religion originated in ancient India.
2. Its adherents sometimes claim to be atheists.
3. Its founder lived in the sixth century BC.
4. The founder wrestled with the problem of human suffering.

5. While sitting under a tree, he experienced "enlightenment."
6. This religion is strong in many Asian countries.
7. It emphasizes compassion for all living things.
8. The southern and northern branches of this faith are Hinayana and Mahayana, respectively.
9. In Thailand, and other countries in South and Southeast Asia, we may see saffron-robed monks of this religion.
10. A Japanese sect of this religion is called "Zen."

2. Who am I?

1. God told me to leave the land where I lived.
2. God told me he would make a great nation and bless me.
3. God changed my name.
4. I helped the servants prepare for a long journey to Canaan.
5. God blessed my husband and me with a son.

Variations: Link onto this example such other activities as these:

1. Divide the group into teams. Present the facts one by one, to the two teams in turn. If one team cannot guess, give the fact to the next team. Continue until one team answers correctly and "wins."
2. Insert a fact which does not belong. Ask learners to identify it.

Purpose: This activity should help learners recall facts and information.

Activity: Ask students to point out a location on a map based on visual or other clues as to what happened there.

Example: Provide for the learners copies of a map of the Middle East. Then ask them to point out locations where the following occurred:

"I am riding in a chariot, reading from a scroll, but I do not understand what I read."

"I was born in a manger here."

"I drove out the money changers here."

"Here a great light made me blind."

"Here I talked with a woman at a well."

"I turned water into wine at a feast here."

"Here I found an inscription, 'to the unknown God.'"

Variations: Link or chain to this example such other activities as these:

1. Ask a learner to identify the person speaking in each case.
2. Ask, What happened immediately before and after these events?

Purpose: This activity should help learners recall facts and information.

Activity: Provide puzzles (or ask learners to design them) which call for the learner to recall certain classes of information.

Example: To teach music facts, draw on the chalkboard a music staff with treble clef. Make a list of several words which use only the letters of the lines and spaces. Draw the notes in place. Ask learners to determine the word involved. (For example: badge, fad, dead, beef, edge.)

ADULTS

YOUTH

OLDER CHILDREN

Variations: Link onto this example such other activities as these:

1. Ask learners to make a list of words on their own. Ask other learners to draw notes in the proper place on the staff to spell the word. This reverses the original plan.
2. Increase the difficulty by accepting only those words which make up a good musical sequence.

Purpose: This activity should help learners recall facts and information.

Activity: Write on cardboard strips the facts or steps in a sequential process (one which involves a certain order). Ask one student to arrange them in order *as the other students instruct him.*

Example: Arrange in random order on a cling chart or hook-and-loop board several word strips which show the steps required for a bill introduced in the House of Representatives to become law. Ask one student to arrange the strips in logical order as instructed by other students. Limit the number of responses one student can make.

ADULTS

YOUTH

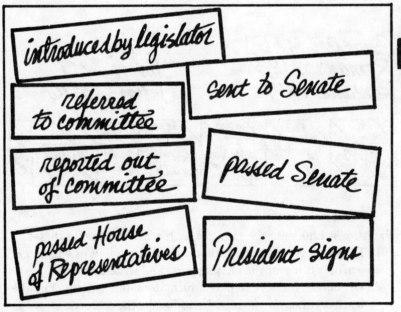

Variations: Link onto this example such other activities as these:
1. After one student places one word strip in the sequence, ask him to call on another student at random to place the next one. He in turn places a word strip and calls on another student.
2. Give one word strip each to several students. Ask them to stand at the front of the room, holding the strips. Ask the remaining students to direct the word strip holders where to stand to create the proper sequence.

Purpose: This activity should help learners recall facts and information.

Activity: Divide into six parts a famous quotation, a Bible verse, or other material assigned for memorization. Rearrange the parts and ask learners to combine the parts to complete the full meaning.

ADULTS

Example: Find six square boxes of equal size. On the top of each box write a part of one of the following Bible verses so that the six segments make up the whole. Select *at random* six other sides. Write a verse on them and so on. Jumble the boxes. Then ask the students to arrange the boxes to display a complete verse.

YOUTH

Genesis 1:1
Romans 3:23
Romans 10:9

Psalm 1:1
John 1:1
John 3:16

Variations: Link onto the example such other activities as these:
1. Deliberately blank out part of several quotations or verses. Let learners discover the missing parts and write them in.
2. Deliberately insert a part which does not belong. Let the learners discover the mistake and make the correction.

Caution: Do not place all the verse parts in the same relationship to each other on the boxes. If you do, *all* verses will appear as complete when the learner does only one of them.

Purpose: This activity should help learners recall facts and information.

Activity: Arrange a game in which the learner is assigned the name of a person, place, or thing—but the learner herself does not know her assignment. All other group members know. The learner tries to identify herself by asking questions or by getting others to tell her some facts which would help her identify herself.

ADULTS

Example: To the back of each learner, attach a placard showing the name of one of the books of the New Testament or the name of a Bible person. Ask the learner to try to find out who she is by asking questions of other persons. When she learns her indentity, she should help others learn their identities.

Variations: Link or chain to this example such other activities as these:

YOUTH

1. Reverse the process. Permit each learner to know his own identity, but supply him with a 3 by 5 card describing, but not naming, another person, place, or thing represented in the group. Ask each learner who has a description to try to "find herself" by locating the person who fits the description.
2. Name "pairs" of persons by whispering to them their names. (For example: Paul and Silas, Jacob and Rachel, Samuel and Eli. Ask persons to locate their "partners" by asking questions.

Notes

1. Adapted from ITT Continental Baking Co., "The Story of a Loaf of Bread," *Teacher,* Vol. 95, No. 8, April 1978, p. 40.

2. Adapted from *Summer Youth Ministry Packet, 1977.* © Copyright 1977 Convention Press. All rights reserved. Used by permission.

3. Edith Shannon, "How Some Teachers Teach Writing," *Today's Education: Journal of the National Education Association,* September 1979. Used by permission.

4. Adapted from "An Experiment in Communication," *Today's Education: Journal of the National Education Association,* September 1969. Used by permission.

5. Adapted from *The Living Textbook, Teacher's Manual,* Fort Worth *Star Telegram,* p. 45. Used by permission.

6. J. W. Pfeiffer and J. E. Jones, *Handbook of Structured Experiences for Human Relations Training,* Vol. 5, University Associates, Publishers and Consultants, 7596 Eads Ave., La Jolla, California, 92037, p. 10. Used by permission.

7. *The Kansas City Star* (Missouri), 1959. Used by permission.

8. From a chapel service, Perkins School of Theology, Dallas, TX, Oct., 1963.

9. Adapted from *Church Staff Relations Kit,* © Copyright, The Sunday School Board of the Southern Baptist Convention. All rights reserved. Used by permission.

10. Marlene D. LeFever, *Turnabout Teaching* (Elgin, IL: David C. Cook Publishing Company, 1973), p. 134.

11. Adapted from "Agape-Christian Lifestyle," Church Services and Materials product, The Sunday School Board of the Southern Baptist Convention.